THE INSIDE JOB

PRAISE FOR SASHA STAIR

"Sasha Stair is on a mission to create more conscious leaders and healthier relationships in and outside of the office. Her debut book, *The Inside Job* is a clear and witty guide for corporate leaders who are ready to reimagine the new wave of conscious leadership. She shares simple, though not easy, transformation tools that leaders at every level can use to align, influence, and motivate individuals, teams, and organizations to achieve massive results."

—**KEITH FERRAZZI**, New York Times #1 Bestselling Author, Founder/Chairman of Ferrazzi Greenlight & Go Forward to Work

"*The Inside Job* by Sasha Stair is a must-read book for corporate leaders at every level. With her engaging wit and candor, Sasha breaks down concepts like authenticity and vulnerability into simple practices that make it possible for leaders to mobilize their teams to achieve extraordinary results."

—**AMY BRANDT**, Former CEO of DocuTech

"*The Inside Job* is the book all corporate leaders need. Faced with so much uncertainty and volatility in today's business world, leaders who are willing to explore their inner world are poised to rise and lead us into the future. Sasha's unique sense of humor—and perspective from within the walls of Corporate America—offers leaders a set of principles to live and lead by."

—**BOB JENNINGS**, CEO of ClosingCorp

THE INSIDE JOB

MASTER THE WORLD WITHIN TO LEAD THE FUTURE OF CORPORATE

SASHA STAIR

Sasha Stair

— is here for you when you need me!

— MB 2023!

Copyright © 2021 by Sasha Stair

All Rights Reserved. Apart from any fair dealing for the purposes of research or private study, or criticism or review, as permitted under the Copyright, Designs and Patents Act 1988, this publication may only be reproduced, stored or transmitted, in any form or by any means, with the prior permission in writing of the copyright owner, or in the case of the reprographic reproduction in accordance with the terms of licensees issued by the Copyright Licensing Agency. Enquiries concerning reproduction outside those terms should be sent to the publisher.

*To my Grandmother, who I fondly called Nana and
Grams. Her intuition guided us both. She believed in me,
always encouraged me to share my stories, and knew I
would be an author long before I did. May you be at peace
in the ocean as the waves carry you to your next
adventure. This one's for you Grams.*

Maluhia and Aloha.

In tribute - Margaret "Margo" Lilian Freeman

July 17, 1921 — October 29, 2021

CONTENTS

Introduction *Brewed with Aloha*	1
1. Flip It and Inverse It *Success Starts from Within*	9
2. Zanshin *A State of Awareness*	25
3. Accept Yourself *Before You Wreck Yourself*	37
4. Attached to Nothing *Connected to Everything*	46
5. Self-Trust *Where Did You Go To, My Lovely?*	59
6. EI *Let's Break Dance*	66
7. Failure *Friend or Foe?*	79
8. Rise with Integrity Through the Real Shit Show	91
9. Leading an Authentic Life	108
10. Leading Yourself First	121
Aloha and Mahalo	129
About the Author	133

INTRODUCTION

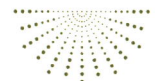

BREWED WITH ALOHA

*P*erhaps you picked up this book because you feel a calling for change in your life, the title caught your eye, or your intuition drove you to grab a copy. Whatever brought you to me and this book, I wish I could sit with you in Maui with a cup of coffee and tell you this story face to face. Alas, the book will have to do, and I am so honored you are reading.

Though most of us resist it, there is change that needs to happen in all of us, and I believe the biggest changes often come to us in the most unexpected packages. For me, that package showed up in the form of a special mentor in a small yoga studio over 15 years ago in one of my favorite towns in San Diego called Del Mar. She would become one of my greatest guides shining light on the path that lie ahead for me. A path dedicated to healing and growth all while still rising to the top in Corporate.

We had just finished a vinyasa class when the instructor announced that Cyndie, a fellow yogi, was going to be hosting a workshop that weekend at the yoga studio on how to discover your true self. I was in my mid-twenties, a successful saleswoman and deep in my masculine energy at that time. I rolled up my mat with conviction and walked up to Cyndie and asked, "So what am I going to get out of this workshop if I come?" My rigid response must have jolted her, yet she smiled, knowing I needed the workshop probably more than any other attendee. I signed up that day. It was a day that changed the course of my life journey forever and started me on what I and many others call "the spiritual path".

In addition to attending the workshop, I signed up for one-on-one coaching thinking I could get some useful tips to put into practice right away. Cyndie had worked in corporate marketing for years and had recently branched off to start her own business with life coaching. She saw right through me from the start. She had known the same type of hardened shell personality from her days in corporate and knew I was going to need "tough love". I remember days where I wanted to quit. Not just give up but throw a temper tantrum and walk out with great purpose, ensuring my melodramatic display had left a lasting impact. But I kept my head and heart in it, and as a result transformed my life. I shifted from being a victim to an empowered leader, from someone who was addicted to chaos to a person who is more centered and calmer. In doing so, I was liberated from the over-stressed life I was living that nearly killed me.

As I embarked on the longest and most important journey of my life, I didn't consciously understand but intuitively knew I would need more than one guide. It took me a few tries, but I found an incredible therapist. I attended self-development workshops and retreats. At the time, I was still very consumed by my father's alcoholism and so a friend introduced me to Al-Anon - a program of recovery for the families and friends of alcoholics, whether or not the alcoholic recognizes the existence of a drinking problem or seeks help. Over time I found mentors in business and people who really showed up for me in life to provide whatever support I needed most, including a place to stay when I was going through any transitions.

Cyndie had spent time living in Maui, and while on the island, she had a deep spiritual connection to the divine feminine and began to feel the ancient wisdom Maui offers pour through her into words, which she turned into her first book. Cyndie would describe how magical Maui was in abstract ways that I couldn't quite digest at the time; Maui's spirit will heal you, the gods/goddesses of the island downloaded divine information to me, and so on. I looked at her like she was bat-shit crazy. How could one place evoke all those ethereal things she was describing and transform a person? Oh, how naive I was at that time.

I was so unaware of how unaware I was. I was completely detached from everything that really matters in this universe and inversely attached to all the objects and things that really don't matter at all. Just before my 30th birthday, I agreed to attend one of Cyndie's retreats on Maui. At that point I had done enough work to know that what you put into something is what you get out of it. So, I committed to myself that when I got to the retreat, I would turn off my phone and computer—all access to life back on the mainland—to allow myself to fully immerse in this experience. The retreat center, Lumeria, has no televisions or phones either, so you are really expected to be present and connected with where you are in the moment. Lumeria is one of the most spiritual and grounded places I have ever visited. The property is like a vortex of spiritual energy, filled with large geodes, ancient tapestries, a large Buddha statue and all the natural wonders of Maui, including banyan trees, hibiscus, bromeliads, bird of paradise, and plumeria. It was the perfect setting to let go of everything I thought I knew about life and open myself up to whatever was going to show up. I was used to stringent and harsh corporate environments, balancing between divorced parents, and being forced to grow up and become independent at a young age. Up until now, everything I had experienced taught me to use logic to solve problems, to let my brain lead the way allowing me to be in full control, and that things were cut and dry. The spiritual path offers a very different picture. You let go and surrender, which at first feels like you are going to lose your mind, and, in the end, you do a bit because you surrender to your heart and intuition allowing your big, beautiful brain to play a supporting role rather than the lead. You listen to yourself (your inner wisdom) and respond from a place of being calm, centered, and emotionally aware rather than reactive and forceful. The beauty of Maui allows this transformation from rigid to soft, controlling to trusting, and reactive to consciously responsive to organically shift within you in a far less intrusive way than being in a corporate conference room.

We were asked to set an intention for the retreat, and I can't remember what intention I set, but I know for sure it was only the tip of the iceberg of what I would come to receive on that truly magical island.

There are so many stories I could share about this one retreat and how much richness I received, but one in particular stands out as the most poignant moment of my life.

One morning, I woke up early. It was still dark outside, but the full, glistening moon was bright enough to light the pathways. I walked over to the kitchen where the chefs were getting a head start on the day's menu, and I grabbed a cup of coffee. I continued down the pathway to the pool area and decided to take a dip in the spa. As I got into the water and settled in, everything became very still and quiet. I looked out over the perfectly imperfect gardens, with all the natural plants growing in their own way. Most mornings the chickens would be there pecking away at seeds, but it was still too early. I sat peacefully in the stillness, and a thought rushed over my body inside and out like a cool breeze that gives you goosebumps. I am all alone. I am not just sitting here alone, I am literally disconnected from all my relationships back home, no calls or texts, no communication or connection back to my life as I knew it before I had arrived on Maui.

At that moment, I felt both terrified and liberated. Could I be alone? Really be alone, fully? Would I be, okay? What if I never got to go back to that same life? Have those same relationships? What if I had to start all over? I had no idea where these feelings and thoughts were coming from, but I chose to surrender and let them pour into me. After the dust of my fears settled and the ripples in the water stopped from my small but frantic movements, I became very still again. And then I heard, "You are and always will be alone on this journey because it is yours and only yours, and you are and will be okay." A deep breath sighed out of me as tears welled up and rolled down my face. For the first time in thirty years, I felt the truth of being still and alone. In the end, it wasn't scary; it was reassuring. To know that though I wouldn't physically be alone for more than probably another hour or so, even if I had to be alone, I would be okay. I would figure things out and keep moving forward because that is life. We can't stop time, we have to keep moving, and we can't really hold on to the past no matter how hard we try, it is really an illusion of the past not the real thing.

Though I would go back to my life on the mainland, it wouldn't be the same life. I would never be the same again. Maui changed me. Because I trusted and opened myself up to receive whatever came up even if it scared me, I was gifted with transformation. I finally understood what Cyndie was talking about. And whether that meant I finally got it, or we were both bat-shit crazy, I didn't really care because I knew Maui was now where my heart would be, and I would come visit her often.

When I decided to write this book, I could think of no better place to begin the journey than back on Maui. COVID-19 travel restrictions were still in effect. It was a last-minute trip, and I jumped through hoops of seventy-two-hour COVID-19 tests, paperwork, masks, the whole nine yards. But I knew I had to go, so I booked the trip and off I went. As I sat one morning at my hotel in the lobby, looking out over Kapalua Bay, feeling the rhythms of the Hawaiian music playing in the background like a soothing lullaby and sipping on my macadamia nut latte, I gazed across the room into the coffee shop and saw a mug that read, "brewed with aloha". How perfect. I opened my computer and started to write. I poured and poured my love—my aloha—into these chapters' week after week, even after I left the island. I bought that mug, two of them, actually. Each morning I pour my coffee into that mug with such gratitude for my guides, my teachers, for the magic of places like

Maui, and the gift I was given to be shown the path and to have the courage to take it.

My wish for you as you read this book is that you too feel the courage to walk that path with me. That you find yourself, your truth, your purpose in a quiet moment when the world stands still for you the way it did for me that morning in Maui. I pray that if you haven't found it already, one day you will feel gratitude and love at a deep, transformative level. Every day you wake, wherever you are, and whatever you are doing, I pray that you brew your morning with aloha. Walk your path with courage knowing it is how you will find all the answers you are looking for, how you will heal from the inside out, and how you will shine your beautiful light. The world needs each of us to recognize the gold that is in each of our stories. That to lead and live with purpose means we must be brave enough to do the inside job and change ourselves first so we may leave a lasting legacy that will become shared wisdom in perpetuity.

1
FLIP IT AND INVERSE IT

SUCCESS STARTS FROM WITHIN

"Your success and happiness lie in you." —Helen Keller

What does having a relationship with yourself even mean? What does a strong and healthy relationship with yourself look like? In all our education, there is little to no education on the answers to these two questions and the tools to help you work through building the foundational elements of managing and leading yourself to success in life.

Well, fear not, because I am going to do my very best to unpack in one book all the life lessons you missed. You will learn:

- How to build strong relationships both inside yourself and with others,
- How to be an emotionally intelligent human and leader,
- How to be self-aware,
- How to work through internal struggles with acceptance,
- How to befriend failure,
- How to listen to and trust yourself,
- How to navigate challenges and setbacks,
- How you can be authentic and true to yourself, and
- How to rise the ranks with integrity without falling prey to corporate politics

I highly recommend you consider grabbing a physical or digital journal for our journey. Often in the book I will reference jotting things down or ask thought provoking questions. Some of my greatest reflections, notes, and ideas are in my journals and I hope you will feel compelled to join in.

I have worked in multiple industries and various roles in my career. I've jumped from corporate to nonprofit, from medical sales to education, from social cause fundraising to consulting, from roles in sales to financial services. I've worked as chief of staff, in client delivery, in IT business operations, and in many oddball jobs in between. In all my experiences both as a young professional and as an executive, nothing has been more important than relationships.

Many talk about the importance of networking, advocating for yourself in a humble way, and paving a path through relationships to get to your life goals. People don't seem to want to talk about how having a healthy relationship with yourself first defines your ability to take those other relationships and your life to their maximum potential.

Professional growth is as much if not more about you than it is about external forces. If you don't have the ability to be self-aware and conscious of how you work, why you work the way you do, what you are good at, what triggers you, and holds you back, you can't move your own success needle. Though it starts with self-awareness, there is so much more to discover in your journey to a healthy relationship with self.

Let's break it down.

SELF-INVENTORY

Let's start with doing some self-inventory. Now would be another great time to grab that journal. Have you ever asked yourself the following questions?

- What is my relationship like with myself?
- How do I identify myself?
- What does my true self look like?
- What brings me joy and purpose?
- How do I feel most days in my life?
- What am I really good at?
- What do I not like to do?

- Where do I struggle and tend to overreact?
- What do I need from myself to be happy and successful?
- What do I think I need from others?

A practice you can start with all these chapters is jotting down, on paper or digitally, your answers to questions and any thoughts that may pop up.

Whether you answer these questions now or not, even just reading them should elicit some type of emotional response. Whether you feel comfortable or uncomfortable, confused, or clear, intrigued, or annoyed, it all means something. And it is worth noting what you are feeling and asking yourself gently, why am I feeling this way?

Typically, when we feel defensive, uncomfortable, or upset in these settings, it is because we are avoiding our truth. If we feel comfortable, at peace, curious, and intrigued it is a sign we may be more aware of our truth and comfortable mostly with where we are in our own journey. If you answered gloatingly, "all positive and nothing to work on with these questions," try again and be more honest with yourself. The only person you are cheating is you. We all have areas for growth, and perfection is a fallacy. Regardless of where you are on that spectrum, the key is to start to get used to introspection and, with great curiosity and no judgment, learn more about where you are today. You may have felt you really knew yourself a few years ago and now as you ask the questions the answers change. Good. Everything changes, all the time. We evolve, we grow, we see and experience things differently, we change our views and perceptions. As we progress in our lives, whether we like it or want to, we change.

WHAT DOES HAVING A HEALTHY RELATIONSHIP WITH SELF MEAN?

The concepts I will share are not new. And yet, they seem to be concepts we struggle to truly understand and put into practice no matter how many times we read or hear about them. Why? My belief is looking in the mirror and recognizing that the one thing we have control over is ourselves may in fact be the hardest part of our journey. Especially when our external world judges us so harshly that if we look in the mirror and see that we aren't "perfect" or "under control" we have somehow failed at life and so why bother trying to address it? It is depressing to think about but it's true. With a framework like that and no tools or indication from the external world that this is something that matters more than what we look like, how high up the corporate ladder we make it, or how perfect our family looks behind that white picket fence, why would anyone ever prioritize having a healthy relationship with self? And yet, it matters greatly that we do. Having a healthy relationship with yourself at its core means healing your wounds, finding, and creating peace and joy from within, and being able to recognize that self-worth is defined from inside yourself not externally.

We teach our children how to do math, explore sciences, learn our history, seek proficiency in languages, even tap into our creative side as we dive into arts and music. Some of our children before becoming adults learn how to balance a checkbook, take care of themselves from cleaning to cooking, fix a flat tire and basic hygiene and health. But when do we teach our children about emotions? About ourselves? How do we see the body that we were gifted in this lifetime? Our relationship to self whether through God, spirit, or your inner voice. These are things we don't talk about, we don't teach, we don't explain, we basically shove it all aside in the hopes that ignoring it will somehow make it a non-issue. Newsflash: ignoring things doesn't make them go away.

What's worse is we are taught to look outside of ourselves for everything. For guidance, for advice, for happiness and peace, for our self-worth, even our purpose. Doesn't that seem a little silly? Not that having a support system isn't helpful. But in the end who knows you better than you?

We must first be willing to recognize that we may have been doing things somewhat backward for some or all our life and accept it knowing we have a choice. With the right lens, tools, and practices you can shift your focus inwards first to ensure that you have created a place of center to operate from go forward. Once you can create equilibrium inside yourself, you can go out and interact with the rest of the world in the most incredible ways. But there is no shortcut for this one. You must turn inwards, heal your wounds, learn to find peace and joy from within, and begin to see that you are worthy of everything you desire.

HEALING YOUR WOUNDS

Before you start to question if you have any, we all have wounds. Certain things people said or did to us changed our perception and distorted how we see ourselves. It could have been a parent, schoolteacher, friend, bully, significant other, boss. Sadly, it is often people we are close to and know well who hurt us. Whether you have had the misfortune of many wounds or are lucky and survived growing up and early adulthood with just a few scratches, we all have wounds that have changed us. We used to believe we were good enough, and now we don't. We thought we were intelligent until someone called us dumb. We thought our ideas were so creative until someone told us they were terrible. We saw our bodies as incredible temples that allow us to do so much until someone physically hurt us and now, we see damaged goods. We believed in the good and thought having a compassionate heart was the best way to be until someone manipulated or took advantage of us and now, we question if people can be good, and we question if we should be so compassionate.

Whatever the story, we all have endured some experience that altered our view of self and most of us created a coping mechanism (i.e., defense tactics, avoidant behaviors, managing chaos, etc.) to manage through rather than heal because no one taught us how to heal emotional wounds. You can't put a bandage on an emotional wound and hope it will heal. Our skin is tougher than our hearts and minds. Instead, we create a hardened shell around our soft hearts to protect us from getting hurt again. We act like we don't care when we really do. We act defensively rather than with an open heart because we know all too well what happens when we open that heart. Some of us turn to more unhealthy and addictive habits because the pain is too hard to face.

Before we go any further, I want you to know that we all do this and it's okay. If no one ever taught us how to understand and process our emotions, how would we ever know how to heal them? We will dive deeper into this subject later in the book but take solace for now in knowing you aren't alone. The world is filled with wounded people. As a result, we have wounded professionals in corporate who behave in emotionally immature ways because they haven't tended to their own needs inside themselves. I can't impress upon you enough how important this one point is. We must heal ourselves first before we can change and heal anyone or anything else, including corporate culture.

As we dive deeper, we will look at different ways to become more aware and in tune with your emotions so you can learn to use them for good rather than in a reactionary way that hurts not only yourself but others too both in and outside of the workplace. For now, I invite you to take note of any stories of wounds that come up for you. Take 5 minutes to jot them down, no need to analyze them at this point. Just taking the first step in being aware that they exist and being able to identify what they are will be critical as we continue our work together.

INNER PEACE AND JOY

Once you have begun your healing process, you will start to discover that some things that used to matter to you no longer hold the same value. We have been taught and shown how peace and joy come from external sources. Our careers, the size of our house, luxurious vehicles, how many likes we get on a social media post, how "picture perfect" our families and stories look, the list goes on and on. When you are laying on your deathbed, what do you imagine yourself thinking about? Whether you got the title you wanted? How many hearts you got on your last Instagram post? No. You will likely be thinking about how grateful you are for the life you lived. Not the life you had—the life you lived. If we are lucky enough to have time to look back on our lives just before we pass, it is likely we will remember the moments that took our breath away, the people that touched our heart in ways you never dreamed possible, the ways we impacted others changing their lives, how fully we lived our purpose, our loved ones, and how happy we are that we got to live this life.

If these are the things we will remember, why not start prioritizing them in your thoughts and actions today? They are what matters. The rest is momentary, fleeting, or even an illusion of what you truly desire. Let me be clear, there is nothing wrong with having goals, a vision board, and dreams you want to achieve. I have many vision boards, and I also have a dream of being on the front of *Forbes* magazine one day. The key is knowing that if it never happens it doesn't matter. It is a dream that opens the possibility and allows whatever is meant to be to attract itself to me. What matters more is, do I live my purpose each day? Do I prioritize the things that really matter at my core; my loved ones (including my fur babies), my calling, my health, changing people's lives for the better, etc. Further, do I find peace and joy from within? Am I able to start my day with a grateful heart and in moments of chaos take a deep breath and remember I am okay, and everything will be, okay?

That type of inner peace and joy is priceless. You can't ask for more out of life if you can find yourself in this place of center, focused on what matters most every day. Bonus, if you can find this secret garden within yourself, the rest of life flows. I wish someone would have explained that to me when I was younger. Perhaps someone tried and I wasn't ready to hear the message or didn't trust them. Regardless, if I would have been able to understand and integrate this practice into my life sooner, I would have avoided unnecessary struggle and suffering. You still must work hard and put in the effort to excel, but there is 100% no need to be a salmon swimming upstream in your career and life. The more I have learned to let go, turn inward and remind myself to focus on living my purpose the more that opportunities in my life and career have shown up without me even trying. Yes, it is really that easy.

If you can get into this flow of living, the universe shows up and provides everything you need. It may not look exactly the way you thought, but if you pay attention, you will start to notice the essence of your dreams, your goals, and your vision board coming true. It is one of the most magical wonders I have ever experienced, and you can experience it too.

SELF-WORTH, SO WORTH IT

I promised to be vulnerable and honest with you, no matter what. So, the truth. Self-worth is the hardest for me. I will share with you my journey and tools to help you along your path while also admitting it is an area I still really struggle with even today. The most critical piece of this puzzle that sadly took me too long to learn is not to give away your power. When we allow others to define our self-worth we have lost. It is that simple. If you have already mastered this, bravo! For the rest of us still battling with this one, let's talk about why reclaiming your power is so vital and how you can begin your journey to taking it back.

Let's explore what giving away your power means and when and why you may have given it away. Giving away your power means allowing someone else to define how you feel about something. In this case your worthiness. It is still a mystery to me if there is one event that started my own doubt of self-worth or if it was a culmination of events over time, but I wouldn't be surprised if it started when I was just 5 years old. Unfortunately, I was molested as a child and though I don't remember exactly how I processed that trauma at such a young age, I can only imagine that somehow, I may have started to tell myself that I and my body were not worthy. If my spirit and body were worthy, I wouldn't have been molested. My parents didn't know, and no one talked to me about it at that age. It wasn't until I was an adult that I talked about it with a therapist and others. So, chances are that for the better part of my childhood, I had given away some of my power and created a story that I wasn't worthy of respect, love, and a life without pain.

Flash forward to my early adulthood and again I found myself in a sexual abuse situation twice over. Even then I didn't connect the dots. People who survive sexual violence but don't heal those wounds can become easy prey for additional violence. Because we already have a weakened image of ourselves, we don't understand that we seek out attention and validation from others. People who are themselves wounded enough to sexually assault another whether consciously or subconsciously can sense an easy way in with someone who has low self-esteem. I know this because of all the studies I read and survivors I spoke with while serving as executive director for Jeans 4 Justice, a nonprofit focused on creating awareness and delivering programs to prevent sexual violence and help survivors heal.

It was hard enough to share my own stories, but it broke my heart into the tiniest particles listening to others share. How many people in our world through sexual or other forms of violence have been emotionally, physically, and spiritually beaten down to a point where they can't see anything good in themselves? Where they doubt if they are worthy of even living let alone if they even want to live after what they have endured?

What's worse, is even if you heal from the trauma mentally and emotionally, the physical impacts can be detrimental to your well-being. I have suffered through years of endometriosis and other ancillary conditions including infertility. These types of inflicted wounds are not something that can be healed overnight, and many people continue to suffer from them even after working through healing modalities.

Though these stories are from my personal life, they are the root of how giving away my power at work has shown up too. Like most, I have worked for bad and good leaders. Every leader has flaws, but some are just bad at leading. And I believe it is probably because they haven't healed their own wounds. One leader, loved to control his leadership team like puppets in his show. We will call him Fred. Fred would manipulate situations to ensure the best outcome for himself and his agenda. When I first started reporting to Fred, I felt like much of my healing journey was completed and I felt strong about my authentic self. But the journey of self-healing never ends and before I could realize it Fred had found ways to pick away at my self-worth. Undermining me in meetings, using me as a "fall gal" or positioning me to manage an area he wanted control over. Whatever his tricks, and Fred had many, they all came at my blind side. I could feel the pain but couldn't quite see what was happening until one day I hit my capacity on jabs from Fred. We had disagreed over the path forward on a key initiative my team was managing. I respectfully pushed back, knowing in my heart my approach was the best direction. Fred didn't take kindly to push back and when he realized instead of "taking orders" I was tired of taking that I now had grown enough confidence back to stand up to him, Fred turned to yelling. I remember sitting in Fred's office in that moment, my head bowed down thinking, "screw this." Instead of saying a word, I just got up, looked him straight in the eyes with a 50% screw you face and a 50% I feel bad for you face and I walked out. What I had been feeling but not seeing was all this time he was using tactics to prey on my weak spots, and I let him take my power away. That day, I took my power back, and I never gave it back again.

Though we would all hope that leaders like Fred just didn't exist. The reality is they do and if you allow them enough space, they will invade, and they will use you for their gain. One of the most critical things I learned from that experience, beyond reclaiming my power, was not to fight back. Fighting isn't the answer either. We must learn to continue to do what we know is right and allow the destiny of those bad leaders to play out in due time. For Fred, and many other bad leaders I had the displeasure of working with, their days were numbered, and something always caught up with them.

Whether you too have a story of trauma or for other reasons have given away your power, it is never too late to start to reclaim it. In many ways, it begins with believing you are worthy of life, of love, of acceptance and of living the life you desire. We all are. Part of what helped me begin to see my worth was admitting that the trauma wasn't my fault. That took a while. For me to admit it wasn't my fault I needed to share my stories more openly with others. I needed to hear other people say it before I could say it to myself. There is nothing wrong with having that support to help you on your journey to self-worth. Just make sure that the people you are letting in are trustworthy and have your best interest at heart, so they offer help rather than create more pain.

I also sought out self-development and healing modalities. I spent time in traditional therapy, I went on self-development retreats, I read books on the subject, went through Al-Anon (12 step program for loved ones of addicts) and many more journeys on my discovery of self-worth. Like I mentioned before this journey is still ongoing for me, but I am in a far stronger place today than I was even 5 years ago. It is a marathon not a sprint and you must be patient with yourself as you embark on the long run. In the end, self-worth will ultimately only be found from within and is critical to your success and well-being in and out of the workplace

Are you starting to feel the theme of this book? Everything we need is within, we must only be brave enough to venture inwards and seek it.

2
ZANSHIN

A STATE OF AWARENESS

"Man who catch fly with chopsticks accomplish anything." —Mr. Miyagi

---

OPEN YOUR SENSES

*A*s you begin this chapter, I invite you to join me in a quick awareness exercise. Before I wrote this chapter I performed the same exercise, and I will walk you through my own experience as an example. It will only take a few minutes but showing you awareness is much more effective than telling you. You'll see.

Find a space where you feel comfortable either sitting with your eyes closed, electronics off, and can be undistracted and focused for a few minutes. I prefer to do this exercise outside. Wherever you are, the key is to quiet your mind and ground. If you are laying down, relax your arms by your side, if you are sitting uncross your legs and find the ground underneath both of your feet. I am going to ask you to close your eyes for a brief time, if you prefer to keep them closed as you complete this exercise then read ahead before you start so you know what questions to ask yourself. Otherwise, you can open them to reference the questions.

Let's begin. Close your eyes and take a few deep breaths. We forget to breathe and hold tight to our air. Now is a chance to remember and to let the air flow freely in and out of your lungs. As thoughts come into your mind, acknowledge them then let them go like clouds drifting off into the sky. Focus on letting everything go and being present to your surroundings. Once you feel calm begin to ask yourself these questions:

1. What do you hear?
2. What do you smell?
3. What do you taste?
4. What do you see?
5. What do you feel?

Gently take note of each answer and really allow yourself to experience the full range of each question.

If you feel compelled, feel free to pause on reading and write about the experience. I have always found journaling to be an insightful tool for us, especially when we are grounded and connected.

If it helps to have an example of what that experience might feel like, here is how it flowed for me:

I hear a variety of birds; the cactus wren, the woodpecker, quail, sparrows all singing their morning songs and almost competing against one another to see who can be the loudest. I hear their wings flapping as they take flight from tree to tree. I hear the cars on the main street not far from our home. I hear a jet trail as he glides through the sky carrying his passengers to their desired location.

I smell the fresh rain that fell last night and the various plants it has brought back to life. It is a smell we don't often get in the desert and so it smells extra divine as I breathe the fresh clean wet air into my lungs.

I taste the remnants of coffee on my tongue. The bitter notes, the smooth and round softness, the nutty flavors.

I kept my eyes closed and saw a mixture of dark and light behind my eyelids. The dark humming while the light tries to break through like rays of sunshine.

I feel the dense humidity of the wet air with a slight cool breeze kissing my skin. I feel warm inside from drinking my coffee and at peace from taking the time to breathe in and become aware of our senses.

Now that you have experienced all your senses, how do you feel? Alive? Awakened? Present? Aware? Does the world feel a little closer to you? Do you notice more once you completed the exercise and opened your eyes? See things differently or notice more detail?

This simple exercise to help you come into your body and become aware of your surroundings is one of the easiest ways to create a state of awareness for yourself. You may be thinking right about now, cool but "so what"? Why does being in a state of awareness matter and how does it help you become more self-aware? When we are fully aware and present, we can respond from a place of consciousness rather than an emotional reaction. We also can pay attention to ourselves more and watch how we respond to things so we can learn more about ourselves – what are our triggers, what are our natural responses, and how does it feel when we get triggered and react? By tapping into this self-awareness, we can become more in tune with ourselves and learn to be more emotionally mature. This wisdom allows us to operate from a place that is serving rather than detracting from our highest good and that of others as well. If we can live a life where we are aware of how our own internal experiences impact our lives and others around us, we can live and lead more consciously and with greater purpose.

CONSCIOUS YET UNAWARE

It seems obvious given how "close" we are to ourselves that we would be able to master self-awareness without much effort. And yet, I have found most people aren't even proficient in being self-aware. The desensitization of our society by external distractions has taken us out of our bodies. Where we as humans may have once turned inward first, we now look externally for guidance, signals, gratification, and acceptance. We have forgotten how to know, listen to, and trust our own bodies, minds, and spirits. We are lost in a sea of over-stimulation, and we must find the courage to bring our ships home from that storm.

I call this state we find ourselves in "conscious yet unaware" or being on autopilot. We know what is going on, but we aren't fully present. Ironically, because we have become so disconnected from ourselves, an easy way to come back to center is to reverse engineer awareness. Beginning with how we interact with the world around us, then connecting to our internal experience. From the exercise we walked through in the previous section, you should be able to feel your senses more finitely. Perhaps prior to tapping into those senses you noticed there were birds in the background, but they were just that, in the background. After awakening your senses, you can now see, hear, feel, taste, and smell more clearly. You have also experienced the magnification of these senses when we engage them together. The more we tap into this state of awareness the more awake and alert we are, picking up on things we may have previously left in the background.

BECOMING SELF-AWARE

Once we can master the practice of being aware, we can begin to pay attention to ourselves. What our natural state of being is, how we respond to things, what patterns we have created, our blind spots, and much more.

Possibly the most poignant reason to learn to become self-aware, is because we can manage the one thing we can control—ourselves. That is a simple concept and a powerful statement. People know this. This isn't frontline news of a new discovery. But, because we were never given the tools to harness skills like self-awareness and conscious leading, we rely more on what we have learned which often includes unhealthy emotional habits stemmed from past traumas, stories, and illusions that have harmed us. Some of us were taught to shove emotions down, not make a big deal out of things, do what is asked of us and who cares what it means or how it feels to you. As a result, part of our population hides from who they truly are and how they truly feel. It creates a self-doubting, masked set of humans trying to make sense of their purpose in life and how they fit in.

Others were given the tools and ability to display their every thought on social media for the whole world to experience. They have learned to accept the illusion of purpose and often self-acceptance through likes and hearts of their posts by others.

Whatever "norm" you grew up with, it is likely some or most of that influencing environment has caused you to hide rather than shine. When all of nature seeks the light, why is it we as humans seek darkness?

We are more aware of how others view us and give little attention to how we view ourselves. We give away our power to others by allowing them to define our self-worth. As a result, what we tend to see is people who look like professional adults in the workplace but are young children inside still experiencing their childhood wounds, stories, and misconceptions.

Let's explore this further and see if anything resonates with you.

- Have you ever felt you were not good enough for a certain job or promotion?
- Do you ever question your abilities or doubt that you may be able to get things done?
- Do you find yourself defending your views and/or approach at work often?
- Do you tend to argue with others or visibly show frustration when people don't agree with you?
- Do you often snap like a short fuse?

If you answered yes to any or all of these, chances are you have unresolved wounds that are repeating themselves in your everyday life.

Pause. Before you take a ride on a defensive or sulking train, take a moment to recognize we *all* have wounds. Even as I write this book, I still have wounds that need healing. It is not a bad thing, but it can be if you aren't aware of them.

Wounds are sneaky little monsters. Often, we believe we have healed them but really, they have shuffled their way into our subconscious making it hard to find or identify them. We must almost become a detective to search for the root cause of our reactions, but if we are willing to do that investigative work the result can pay dividends for our success at work and our inner peace and joy in life.

INSPECTOR GADGET

I like to think of becoming self-aware as embodying Inspector Gadget. If you are unfamiliar with the reference, *Inspector Gadget* was a 1980s animated show that starred none other than Inspector Gadget himself. The inspector was quite the dichotomy of a character; filled with intelligence and compassion while at the same time a little clueless and gullible. He had all of these "gadgets" at his disposal to help him solve the crimes but was a little clumsy in leveraging them. Enter stage right, self-awareness. We are all filled with tools to be self-aware but sometimes we are a little clumsy like Inspector Gadget trying to get our footing under us as we figure it out.

Fear not, just as Gadget had a knack for stumbling upon the answers to each mystery, we too have all the tools we need to find our way through our inner adventure to becoming more self-aware. So how do we employ those tools to solve the mystery?

I find a good place to start is humility. We must first be willing to admit to ourselves where we may be behaving in a way that is unbecoming of our true selves. For me, in my early twenties I was extremely defensive in both my personal and professional life. At the time, the underlying wound had shuffled its way into the archives of my brain. But if I had been willing then to look closer, what I would have found was a young woman who was sexually abused and in one instance froze and in another fought back unsuccessfully. Through those traumas, I had built a defense mechanism to protect myself but because I was unaware of this coping method it ended up hurting me not protecting me. I was so hurt inside and couldn't see it. Any small comment that was slightly offensive would set me off and though my wit was compelling the harsh nature of my comments was quite less so. I was tough as leather on the outside and crumbled to pieces on the inside.

During that time, I was a medical device sales rep, and I was good at my job. I'd like to say that most of my success back then was due to my natural skills but sadly I think just as much of it was because I was so determined to "beat" everyone else and win. What was I even competing for? But this is what unhealed wounds look like. We fight, we push, we overdo it. Whatever it takes to prove we are "okay", or we are even better than okay we are invincible! Bullshit. No matter how good we are, or how close to superman or wonder woman, in the end we are still human.

I recall a client at that time, a thoracic surgeon in California, having coffee with me one day to discuss an upcoming case where he had planned to use one of my company's stents. After finishing our talk regarding the case, he asked if he could offer some advice. Eager to please my clients I leaped at the chance to hear what he had to say. "You know, you are really good at what you do, but you'd be unstoppable if you would soften a little." Enter stage left, my inner dialogue: I'm sorry, what did he just say? Soften? What the heck are you talking about, *soften*? Do you think I got to where I am by being soft?

Looking back, I laugh at this story because he was oh so right and I was oh so oblivious. I had hardened on the outside. What I hadn't realized at that point in time was how much I had forced myself to be in my masculine energy and had completely forgotten I was even a woman with oodles of feminine energy left idle.

Eventually, through therapy, an incredible life coach and a lot of self-realization I was able to see more clearly how past wounds were impacting my life including that one. Let me forewarn you now, when you realize that the only person holding you back from changing these things is you...gulp. That is the hardest pill to swallow. How could someone else hurting me ultimately mean I am responsible for changing?

But here we are full circle. Becoming self-aware allows us the opportunity to change the one thing we can control: ourselves. As you start to explore the behaviors you may currently or previously displayed that are not the "true" you, be compassionate with yourself. It isn't shocking that we go into a mode of self-protecting even if it doesn't really work. It is only natural for us to want to forget, hide, or erase the events and circumstances of life that have hurt us.

The golden nugget is in how we choose to respond once we become aware of how we react to these situations. If we choose to use them as wisdom and power to help make us better humans and leaders, we too can save the day like Inspector Gadget.

DID IT WORK?

So, did I soften, and did it work? Yes, and yes.

What is important though is not that I needed to soften but rather that I was eventually willing to have enough humility to look within and start to unravel the illusion I had created for myself. What I found through that discovery was "soften" to me meant tapping more into my feminine energy to balance the immense masculine energy I had grown so accustomed to.

Whatever the behavior and the wound, it will look different for each of us. The key is to be willing to explore and learn more about yourself. Because I chose to journey down that road less traveled, I have become a better influencer, a stronger negotiator, a more compassionate manager, and a more joyful spirit that emanates a whole lot of light. Just ask my colleagues, they often wonder where all the sunshine comes from. Rainbows, of course. Magical unicorns and rainbows, my friends.

3
ACCEPT YOURSELF

BEFORE YOU WRECK YOURSELF

"Self-acceptance is truly a heroic act." — Nathaniel Branden

*A*ccepting ourselves as we are might be one of the most challenging tasks we face in life. Unless you are a complete narcissist and sociopath, we all have things we don't like about ourselves. Our looks, our decisions, our lives. What's unfortunate is we often spend more time focused on those negative outlooks, which pale in comparison to how much beauty we bring to this world.

Now that you have begun the process of becoming more self-aware, you will start to see those flaws as you reflect, as you look in the mirror, and as you start to truly identify with who you are at your core. As you continue this journey, I invite you to take the role of observer rather than judge. This process of introspection isn't meant to make us feel bad about ourselves and where we are in life. It is meant to simply be an opportunity to see more clearly, to learn more about ourselves so that we might have the chance to redirect or stay the course as we see fit.

I struggle with self-acceptance both personally and professionally. As a child, my grandmother, who was a model and fashion designer, used to measure me every time I visited her. She would pull out her sewing tape—the long soft measuring tape—and wrap it around my scrawny little legs, my waist, my bust as it slowly grew, my hips. I remember her being so proud when I reached 18 years of age and I had finally hit her perfect measurements; the ideal model 34, 24, 34 as she called it, or my bust, waist, hip measurements. She even took me to a modeling agency at the time that handed me a contract stating if I changed size even a quarter of an inch or gained more than or lost more than one pound, the contract would be void. I walked away from that disgusting opportunity.

For my grandmother, that was her world. She didn't understand—or at least, I hope she didn't comprehend—the damage that she was doing to my psyche. I am nowhere near those measurements now, at almost forty years of age, nor do I aspire to ever be again. Sadly, however, the days of her expectations have not left me. I still look in the mirror and judge myself. Clothes don't feel like they flatter me, and I throw them on the ground with distaste for my imperfections. It is ridiculous. Outright ridiculous, and yet, it is part of who I am.

We started fertility treatment last year, and the journey has been treacherous. At first it turned my body image issues into a glorified horror story. Then came a day when I realized my body is a temple that can grow life. How can I possibly judge how it looks when its purpose is in what it does for me and this world? That day shifted my perspective and has helped me heal part of that self-image wound. But I won't lie, it is still an ongoing battle I face each day with as much acceptance and grace as possible.

Similarly, in the workplace, I self-doubt to the point of negating anything poignant that comes out of my mouth. I think we are so scared of being judged for being "wrong" or people not understanding us that we ultimately "box" our sentences. We share our thoughts and add a preface, "I'm not an expert but..." or we add a closing statement, "but I could be wrong, or perhaps there is a better way." No one is 100% an expert, and we can all be wrong at times, and there are always better ways. So why do we add the obvious statements that pick away at our brilliance?

We are so scared to take that self-awareness and accept ourselves for exactly who we are today. Not who we were yesterday, or who we aspire to be tomorrow, but who we are right now. When are we going to look in the mirror and not just tell ourselves but actually believe that in this moment we are enough just as we are?

News flash: there is only one YOU. Instead of trying to be someone else, imagine what it would be like, feel like to own who you truly are? Let's stop robbing the world of the unique gifts we each bring to the table. Stop trying to convince ourselves we need to be different or somehow aren't good enough. We are all doing the best we can with what we have at any given moment.

Does that mean we don't strive to grow and improve? Of course not. It just means we don't discredit ourselves for where we are today because we already have a lot to offer, just as we are. So how do we do that? How do we accept ourselves, deal with self-judgment, and keep our egos in check while confidently owning our greatness?

ACCEPTANCE STARTS WITH HONESTY

In order to truly accept ourselves, we have to be honest. Maybe you aren't ready to share your deepest, darkest concerns with the rest of the world, but you have to admit them to yourself. If we can't be honest with ourselves, we can't work on being a better version of ourselves.

Being self-aware and accepting yourself are like salt and pepper. They complement one another and travel together. Sometimes, things we are good at can also hurt us, but if we are aware of those attributes and we accept them, we can harness the power of choice in how we continue to live out our lives with those attributes.

For instance, I read people really well. It is a great attribute and one I didn't realize I was so good at until more recently. Very often my intuition about people is spot on. However, sometimes that read means I see someone's potential flaws and quickly judge what I think they will do with that flaw, which is quite frankly none of my business and is unfair. Let's use an unharmful example, my cat Little Man. I know this cat. He is a stubborn, independent little shit. He doesn't like to cuddle, so I just expect him to run away every time I try. I judge that based on what I've seen out of him, he will always run away. But at times he doesn't. He leans in and nuzzles his head into you and reminds you he does love you and most likely won't kill you in your sleep.

What we can learn from this scenario is twofold: not only is my cat not predictable in how he behaves, but my judgment of him isn't always accurate. I know it is a silly example, but if I judge someone in the workplace in a way that sets an expectation that they will always behave a certain way because they usually do, I don't leave them space to change. It sounds like I have more control over the situation than I do, but I believe in energy and holding space for people. Giving them the benefit of the doubt while still keeping my eyes open and not turning a blind eye. But at times I don't always embody that, and I must be honest with myself where that could be hurting not just my own leadership but other people as well.

No pity party, no harsh judgment, just awareness of an opportunity for me to shift how I handle things.

To accept that there is nothing wrong with me for acting that way while also recognizing I have a choice to behave differently, which could make a positive impact in many lives, including my own.

Self-acceptance is so beautiful in that way. As we learn to accept ourselves, we naturally accept others more as well. What a gift.

HOW TO NAVIGATE THE SELF-JUDGMENT

As we continue our Inspector Gadget series, fumbling our way through this self-exploration, it will be challenging to not get down on yourself. You may feel foolish for not realizing things sooner or feel like you're a terrible person for not doing better. But that is not the point. The point is to become aware, accept things just as they are, then decide what you want to do next. Life is all about a series of decisions that lead us down paths that ultimately weave the tapestry of our lives.

Just like other artists, you are allowed to reuse your canvases. Paint over them. Start anew. However you choose to paint your story is up to you. But you can't move forward if you are too busy dwelling on your past. So when you start to unpack your past patterns and your behaviors, here are some tips to consider to help you not go down Wallowing Lane.

1. Judgment is a natural human tendency. There is no point in trying to avoid it. The

key is to acknowledge it, let it guide you, and move on.
2. No one really likes to roll around in their own "poo." It's smelly and gross. So don't do it.
3. Don't underestimate the power of self-compassion. Look in the mirror, write it down, whatever works for you—repeat over and over until it sinks in "we are all doing the best we can in any given moment with the tools we have."
4. Don't be afraid to ask yourself, do I have the tools I need to be the person I truly want to be? If not, where can I find them or who can help me identify them?
5. If something is really bothering you and you feel guilty, shameful, or lost with a scenario, give yourself time to process through it. There is no way around things we must go through. So take your time. There is a difference between rolling in your poo and truly moving through pain, discomfort, and judgment to a place of healing.
6. Surround yourself with a support system; people who you love and trust, environments that make you feel safe and happy, take a walk through nature and let it cleanse you.
7. Write down a list of all the things you self-judge and draw a line down the center of the page. On the opposite side write positive affirmations you can say to yourself instead. Our thoughts become reality, use this activity

as an opportunity to shift them from judgments to motivations.
8. I know it's cliché, but it is SO true that someone always has it worse and there is always something worth living for.
9. Remember you are not alone. We all do this. Even just accepting that will help you on your journey to self-acceptance.
10. Don't let the darker sides of you define you; let them illuminate you.

BEING ALL IN

Acceptance means being willing to accept all of you and all things in life. It can't just be the parts you like. We all have darkness and light inside of us. We shouldn't be afraid of the darkness. It gives our lives texture and color. Often the insights we gain from the darkness; our struggles, failures, mistakes, and mishaps are what help us define our light. It guides us to how we want to take on the next chapter in our life. It gives us the choice to change. It reminds us that nothing is static or stays the same. Life is always evolving; we are always changing.

Through my work with sexual violence survivors, I often heard so many of them say they wish the trauma would have never happened. For me, it was also a struggle until I realized one day that if I had never experienced the trauma, I might not have been able to help people through their stories with the same impact. It sounds terrible, but my trauma gave me purpose in life to help others. One story at a time, if I can help make someone's path to healing easier, then I have lived a life of purpose.

The same is true in the workplace. I have dealt with some terrible circumstances and people. Those adversities forced me to sit through uncomfortable situations, to learn when and how to stand up for myself, and how to navigate the delicate nature of politics. No matter how much we wish these adversities and politics didn't exist, the truth is, they do. Learning to accept them sets us free from the entrapment of thinking we can stop them.

I once had a mentor tell me, "If you don't like politics, don't get your hopes up about being an executive because they only get worse as you move to the top. Instead, try to find something you can do to turn them into a positive." I can and do choose to accept corporate the way it is—at least for now. I also chose to accept that how I operate is often in direct contention with how most corporations operate today. Accepting that difference set me free to see another way. If I want to change corporate, it starts with me. Accepting myself for all that I am and finding ways to spread my light so others can do the same. I won't lie; I have an ulterior motive. My hope is that one day, my internal transformation and sharing will inspire others to heal themselves from the inside out so that we may start to in turn heal corporate from the inside out too. But it starts with each of us, so are you in?

4
ATTACHED TO NOTHING

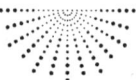

CONNECTED TO EVERYTHING

"The root of suffering is attachment." —*The Buddha*

If you would have asked me to comprehend the statement "Attached to nothing, connected to everything," even 15 years ago I would have looked at you with a very confused face. How can I be connected but not attached to something? And are we talking about physical attachment? Emotional? Mental? Yes. One of the first books I ever read on my spiritual journey is, "The Untethered Soul." This book literally changed my life but not right away. Initially I was baffled. Not because the concepts didn't make sense but because it was as if someone took my entire life and turned it on its head. I had been living my life in the complete opposite way - connected to nothing and attached to everything.

When I talk about connection in this context, I am referring to having and feeling a relationship to something without being linked to it in perpetuity. Meaning, I can have a purposeful relationship or connection with someone or something for any amount of time but not be attached to that person or thing forever. For example, I can be on a hike and walk past a tree and stop to take in its beauty, its wisdom, and its power. I can stand there hugging it, touching it, or just observing it and appreciate its magnificence. The number of years it took to grow tall, the storms it survived to stand strong, the protection it provides to animals. I can take in all this wonder, acknowledge its magnificence, say thank you and walk away perhaps never remembering that exact tree in that exact place. Feeling no desperate need to go back and find that exact tree again. Trusting that the connection formed in that moment was meaningful and whether our paths cross again or not, I have been impacted by this experience. That is connection without attachment.

That's great, but it is a tree. What about our relationships with people, which can be far more complex? Let's start with a professional relationship. I worked for someone once that was my polar opposite. Let's call this person Sally. For the first few years, being like a chameleon, I did everything in my power to adjust how I showed up in the workplace to try and find equilibrium with Sally. I also held hope that over time I could influence Sally to see that my style of leadership was something that could help her in being successful if she was willing to change. If Sally wasn't willing to change, then perhaps she would at least see the complement of our styles as a needed balance for the organization. What I didn't realize I was doing was setting an expectation that things would turn out the way I wanted - though well intended, it was selfish - and I became attached to the outcome that Sally would either change or find balance in our complementary styles.

As a result, I spent those first few years working for Sally in agony. Even after years dedicated to shedding the "people pleaser", the remnants of that side of me were still present. I tried every trick up my sleeve, every tactic I could drum up to help change the situation. I created events that allowed Sally's personality to come forward so people could see who she really was and not just the tough shell that she portrayed. I took the beatings in meetings and behind doors with as much grace as I could stomach. I would take "hard conversations" out of the office and have them over dinner and wine, hoping the more relaxed setting would help ease the discussion. I cleaned up the collateral damage from Sally's outbursts and self-serving political moves. No matter what I tried to help Sally see her leadership style was in most people's view antiquated and harsh, in the end Sally wasn't going to change, nor admit she needed to. She was also never going to fully understand or be able to accept our differences. In truth, though I didn't agree with Sally's style and approach, it wasn't my job to change her nor judge her as being wrong. It was my job to learn and then decide what was best for me.

I wasn't ready to give up on the professional relationship, but I also recognized I couldn't keep exhausting myself trying to reach untenable expectations. So, I let go of the expectations of myself and Sally. I committed to focus on what I believed in my heart was right regardless of the consequences. When I lovingly detached myself from the unhealthy expectation of what the relationship "should" have been, everything changed.

Now don't get overly excited because it got worse before it got better. I make this point rather than hide from it because I believe it is one of the reasons people don't let go of attachments. We get so comfortable with what we know. When we finally have the courage to stand in our truth and things get tough our natural instinct is often to retreat to our comfort zone. It is such an easy thing to do, and we have all done it so don't feel bad. However, it is the definition of living a cyclical yet static life. Continuing to repeat the cycles of trying to break free only to return to where you started, is exhausting and leaves us unsure if we can try again. It borders the line of insanity, trying the same thing over and over expecting a different result. If we truly want to create change, we must focus on ourselves. We must find the tenacity and grit to push through the discomfort especially during those moments where we think we aren't strong enough to do so.

When it came to Sally, I began to stand in my truth and speak truth to power. I no longer allowed Sally to control my teams. I made it very clear they took direction from me not her and that if she had concerns to take it up with me. I also started calling her out on poor behavior. When she would yell at me, I would stand up and say, "I don't deserve nor do I accept this behavior," as I quietly walked out of the room. The response from my boss was direct outrage combined with passive aggressive moves. It was unacceptable that I was pushing back, even though I was respectful in how I challenged her views and approach. If I wasn't a "yes woman" I was a "no woman." There was no consideration, no in between, and no respect for my thought leadership. To that person, I was being insubordinate and a nuisance. As a result, what used to be terse quips here and there now turned to curt comments, snide hurtful remarks, and even more yelling. Sadly, I wasn't the only leader on Sally's team who endured these antics. I watched as my other colleagues experienced the same treatment, unless they were willing to be a "yes man" in which case they were praised for their behavior, especially when it was unprofessional but made our boss look good.

There came a day when enough was enough. I wasn't going to back down, but I also knew continuing to be at odds with this person was only going to make both of our lives miserable. I will never forget the days leading up to that inflection point for me. There were so many events that compounded into my decision to stop trying and to look for another job. Asking me to make an unethical decision, berating me in their office with the door open for everyone to hear, an annual review that quite frankly included slander, the list went on and on. I had hit my breaking point. No one should ever have to endure a situation like this but unfortunately many do at one or many points in their career.

Because I had let go of my attachment to the relationship, to my unrealistic expectations that I could ever help change the situation or the person, it was much easier for me at that time to walk away. It didn't happen as fast as I would have liked and I had to grit my teeth and have patience until a new opportunity came along, but I persevered through that trying time.

When we get attached to a specific outcome such as changing another person, changing a company, or whatever the example may be, I promise you it never ends well. We try to control and command which constricts and restrains both our and others' abilities to change. There is no space for change when things are so tightly held. We must learn to not cling on to things, situations, and people. Nothing will ever remain the same, even relationships evolve over time so trying to "attach" and "hold on" in truth is a fallacy because your relationship yesterday is not what it is today. And last I checked, no one has figured out how to go back into time except maybe Michael J. Fox and Christopher Lloyd.

DEVELOP YOUR CONNECTION SKILLS

Being connected is how we relate to things in this world, it is how we experience bonds, feeling of shared life, and often is what gives us purpose. Creating connections, being connected, and learning how to connect at different levels is a critical skill set to rounding out your inner world.

Some people are experts in this area and know exactly how they connect with people, nature, experiences. Others may be unsure or think I am talking in gibberish. Wherever you fall on that spectrum, let's walk through a quick assessment to give yourself an "insider" look into how you experience connection.

Answer the following questions and take note in the book or in your journal, especially pay attention to random thoughts that come to you (hint: they aren't so random). Jot them down without analyzing them.

1. When you see a bird in your yard, what do you do?
a) Nothing.
b) Smile and possibly think how beautiful s/he is.
c) Get curious what the bird is up to.
d) Shoo it away so it doesn't poo on your car or deck.

2. Which of the following is true when you look in the mirror, not to see how you look for the day but to really look inside yourself?
a) You feel good about yourself, like you do the best you can each day.
b) You feel disappointed, angry, shameful, or another negative feeling.
c) You think you are the shit and nothing about you could be better.
d) You see good and opportunity for things to improve.
e) You have a blank face and can't think of anything off the top of mind.

3. On a scale of 1–10 how would you rate your ability to connect with each of the following:
a) Yourself
b) Other people
c) Animals
d) Nature

Some insights for you to consider based on your answers.

For #1, if you answered A, you are either avoiding the real answer, which could be a sign that you are avoiding connection, or if that is truly how you feel, you may be more disconnected than connected. If you answered B or C, you connect with other life, and you feel things, which is a sign that you have some form of connection to that life (whether a plant, animal, etc.). If you answered D, you are connected but may be either in the moment just annoyed with the bird or you could be missing an opportunity to connect at a deeper level.

For #2, if you answered A, B, or D, you in some ways are connected to yourself. You aren't scared of looking inwards and having the courage to see what is light or dark. You feel a sense of awareness and understanding of where you are in life and you may have an opportunity to connect further, but you are at least showing signs that you know how to connect with yourself. If you answered C, you either are making a joke of this exercise or may need to eat humble pie. We may know our strengths and exude confidence, but no one is the "shit" or has nothing to work on. Try again. If you answered E, chances are you are avoiding or don't know how to have a connection to yourself. I highly recommend you try looking in the mirror and asking yourself the same question every day until your answer changes.

For #3, use this to evaluate if any are less than a 5. If they are, it might be worth exploring if there is anything there to be uncovered. Perhaps a past trauma or experience that left you uncomfortable with a person or animal. Or an accident in the ocean or on a mountain that left you fearful of something in nature.

With each question, this an opportunity to discover and notice without judging. How we connect or disconnect from things can be very telling. You can then determine if you feel good about where you land on the scale for each or if there may be areas where you want to dive deeper, heal, or make a change.

If you want to work on your ability to connect, below are some tips to consider:

1. When you are in a conversation with someone, put your phone and any other distractions aside and really focus on the person. Make eye contact, let them know you are listening. Often, we listen to respond, if you truly want to connect with someone listen to understand and build empathy.

2. Go out into nature - whether a hike or even just your backyard. Find something to focus on - a bird, a tree, a flower, the sky - anything that is living and part of nature. Spend time observing the bird, what does the bird look like, how big is it, what is it doing, is it a mother with a nest to go back to? Be inquisitive and just observe. If you're an artist perhaps you draw the bird, tree, or flower. Perhaps you write a poem. Or perhaps you just sit and watch really focusing on that one thing.

3. Spend time with a pet or if you don't have one go to an adoption center for an hour. Again, put all distractions aside and just be with the animal - hold him, snuggle her, play with a toy - observe the animal's response to you - how the animal will naturally connect with you.

Connection is all around us. It is always available to us, and we naturally want and need connection as humans. Connection is a part of who we are and how we exist and thrive in this world. The more you connect to yourself and everything in the world around you, the more compassionate, understanding, grounded, and insightful you will become. You will also find more meaning in life, particularly the "little things" that we think aren't that important but are some of the greatest wonders this planet has to offer.

FREE YOURSELF FROM ATTACHMENTS

Now that hard part—how do I detach from things and how do I consciously choose to not attach? I have no idea. Good luck. Kidding. But it is not an easy exercise, however, the more you learn to do it the easier it gets and the faster you notice when you are creating attachments.

Let's start with why we attach ourselves to things and people. For starters because it is cozy and comfy to get used to things we like. It is easy, we know the thing or person, mostly we know what to expect - no surprises, and it feels stable and steady. For example, I love my house - it is my sanctuary and one of my favorite places to center. Let's compare attached versus unattached with this example. If I attach myself to my house, when the market goes up and we have equity in the home and the most fiscally intelligent thing to do is sell, I can't because I have grown too attached to the home and don't feel I could survive without it. Where would I go to center and ground? What if my new home doesn't feel like a sanctuary? Exhibit A, unhealthy attachment.

Now let's say, the home is still the same - a place I love, I ground and center in, I have made my sanctuary. And I also find peace centering on the top of a mountain or on my yoga mat. I find sanctuary at spa, on a hike, or inside of my heart. We've decided the best decision is to sell our house. Do I feel some form of pain and sadness letting go, of course I do, I am not perfect with attachments, and I also feel connected to my home which is perfectly fine? However, it is much easier to let go. I trust that I can find a new home, I know I have other places to ground and make sanctuary, and in the end the house is just a house, what we do with the house and bring into the house is what makes it a home and we can make a home anywhere. Exhibit B, healthy detachment.

It becomes more complicated with people, particularly those we love, but the more we can do to lovingly detach ourselves from "needing" a person the healthier it is for us and for the relationship. When we cling too tightly, again there is no room for the relationship to grow. When we feel like we can't survive without the other person, we can start to form unhealthy codependences that are far more complicated to untangle. Being unattached to a loved one doesn't mean you aren't connected, in a relationship and/or deeply care for and love the person. It just means you have a healthy relationship that can grow and flourish naturally. That can ebb and flow through an ever-changing life without rigid restrictions. It also gives you permission to let go when the time comes. And it will come; whether you choose to end the relationship or life on this earth ends, the relationship in physical form will eventually depart because that is life. Being as unattached as possible only makes the life we share with people more enjoyable and though it can't take away the pain of losing a loved one it can help you find and make peace with the inevitable.

It may seem sad, but it doesn't have to be. If we can see this chapter for what it is, we can liberate ourselves to live a more healthy, joyful, and purposeful life. Being unattached frees us from the self-inflicted pressures to be a certain way or to force outcomes we can't control. Connection is what saves us. It is what creates the healthy bonds we need to bring us together on this journey in a loving way. To stop arguing, trying to be right, and make a point and shift us to a place of understanding, reason, and perhaps even an ability to use our intelligence combined with our compassion to solve big problems at home, in the office, and in our world.

5
SELF-TRUST

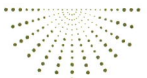

WHERE DID YOU GO TO, MY LOVELY?

"As soon as you trust yourself, you will know how to live." —Johann Wolfgang von Goethe

---

Where and when did we lose our way? Was it from the beginning of time? Was it when man first faced war? Was it when policy makers took their first bribe, or a CEO made his/her first million after skirting the law?

We could debate that question for hours, not that we would want to, but the question begs another more relevant question for our time together: "When did we lose trust in ourselves?"

Was it when we asked the person out in middle school and got rejected? When we asked for what we really wanted for our birthday and didn't get it?

When we took that job that looked so much greener only to find out the grass was fake?

Somewhere along the way we lost our ability to self-trust, to look inward, to really listen and to follow the guidance of our intuition, our higher knowing, our gut. Without leaders having a sense of self-trust, corporations stand no chance of having employees who will help change the way we lead and the way we live.

We live in a society where any failure seems to be blasted all over the front page of the news. And in a world where that is true, who would put themselves out there? Why would you trust yourself when the one time something goes wrong the whole world laughs at you, like that time you fell at school as a kid and everyone was watching.

We have created such a cruel and unusual environment for the power of our inner wisdom to come to fruition. In fact, we have made it so painful that even the words inner wisdom makes some people shutter. It is a deep suffering that I believe sits at the root of our most damaging wounds in this world.

If you can't have trusting and healthy relationship with yourself first, then you can forget having successful relationships elsewhere.

I learned this lesson the hard, arduous, knock you down the stairs kind of way both in personal and professional settings. In my personal life it took one failed relationship after another until I ended up at the ultimate low. As a survivor of sexual assault and violence, I never imagined I would end up in a relationship with someone who would bull doze through the boundaries I had worked so hard to create. But I did. I'll never forget the irony of the whole thing. At the time I was in therapy, continuing to heal from my past traumas and my therapist broke protocol to tell me, "If you don't leave, he will eventually kill you, maybe on purpose, maybe by drunken accident, but regardless of how or why it will happen, and you need to leave." Another person might have heard those words and immediately gone home and packed their bags, right? I had worked with this therapist for years, and I trusted her. I knew I needed to hear the jolting message, but it still was not enough to shake me.

Around that same time, I had also been speaking at San Diego State to the leaders of their fraternities and sororities. Specifically, I worked with them within a program focused on educating Greek leadership about the importance of sexual violence prevention. I absolutely loved speaking at these sessions every semester and I was also terrified every time I had to share. Each semester was a different group of leaders, and every semester I both had to relive my multiple experiences of sexual violence while also receiving the opportunity to heal those traumas further.

One afternoon just a few weeks after my therapist had jolted me with her poignant and vital words, I found myself sharing with the sorority leaders about what I was going through. "After everything I have gone through, everything I have done to help myself heal and create healthy boundaries, how the heck did I end up in an abusive relationship? And worse, how can I sit here in front of all of you and ask you to be different when I can't even do it for myself?"

It was at that moment that I realized the hypocrisy of it all. Here I was teaching and facilitating what it meant to have a healthy relationship with yourself, and others and I hadn't even really broken free of what held me back from a healthy relationship with myself.

The young women in the program surrounded me with so much love and reflection that I so desperately needed. They were bold and forward in their words. "You don't deserve this, you need to get yourself out of this situation, you need to take care of YOU." What I realized in that moment was not only did these young women hold no judgment against me for still being in the "process," but their youth still offered a strength that even only being 10 years their senior, I had lost.

You see, the older we get and the more experiences we have, the wiser or more wounded we become. The choice is ours.

What the heck does this have to do with how you lead in corporate?

Well, my friends, let me tell you.

WHAT DOES NOT TRUSTING MYSELF LOOK LIKE IN THE WORKPLACE?

Do you ever catch yourself questioning whether you should share something in a meeting? Doubting a decision, you made? Belaboring what you said or did in a meeting for days after it happened trying to figure out why it happened and how you could have prevented it?

All these forms of questioning and doubt are signs of a lack of self-trust.

At some point in your career, you reached a threshold where you stopped sharing your authentic wisdom and started censoring your thoughts, your intuition, and as a result, your behaviors. Something has caused you to be gun shy and is holding your greatness back from being brought forth into corporate and the world. Now let's be honest, there are people who are the counter to this, and it seems like their mouths are always open and you'd put money on them choking on a fly. Whether you are the self-questioner or the over talker, neither gets you to trusting your wisdom and using it for good.

For many in corporate it seems logical that not speaking up or speaking up too much can be a problem. But what people don't seem to grasp is, it isn't about how and when you speak up. It is ALL about where you speak from. We'll come back to that concept in a minute.

Think back to a time when you felt really strong about making a decision and things went in your favor. Perhaps it was bringing up an idea you had in a meeting, creating a new organizational structure for your team, or going toe to toe with a colleague on a matter you knew required resolution. Whatever the situation, I want you to visualize it in your mind. Where were you? Who was with you? What was the setting? Really bring yourself back to that time and place. Now start to recall the moment that the idea was accepted, your project was approved, you resolved a huge conflict. Whatever the positive result, it worked out and you felt really good inside. Why? Because you trusted yourself, your inner wisdom, and you made it happen.

Now think of the inverse, a time when you said something or brought an idea up and someone shot you down in a meeting, embarrassed you in front of others, or made your idea seem like it was the most asinine thing like a screen door on a submarine (my husband, a former submariner gave me that one). At that moment, how did you feel? I'm guessing pretty bad. You may have clammed up, felt angry or frustrated, you may have told yourself "Never again!" or just questioned yourself pragmatically, "was it a bad idea? Am I off my rocker?" Whatever the case, it is in moments just like these that we break down the essence of our self-trust.

I consider myself pretty good at taking the self-criticism, self-judgment, and questioning and processing it to the point that I regain my self-confidence and get back on the horse. But even then, a little chip still exists in my self-trust. Why? Because we put too much value in the opinions of others rather than in the wisdom within ourselves.

That stops now. To lead yourself, to change how we lead in corporate, and to move us from a place of greed, politics, and games to a world of emotionally mature leaders we must first learn to change our relationship to self. This doesn't mean we stop caring about make a living and being successful but what changes is we don't allow those desires to be at the cost of being a good leader. And being a good leader starts within yourself. Being a good leader is having the courage to love and accept who we are and the unique gifts we bring to this world, then trusting ourselves to express those gifts.

When we learn to trust ourselves, and to speak and act from a place of trust, love, and acceptance the words that flow from our mouths, the decisions that we make and the behaviors we display shift.

6
EI

LET'S BREAK DANCE

"In a very real sense we have two minds, one that thinks and one that feels." —Daniel Goleman

---

Once you release self-doubt and have returned to a place of trust, your thoughts and words become more aligned to your true self. The tricky part is sometimes our true self is in a state of frustration, anger, or other emotionally charged energies. With self-trust under your belt, you can now harness that power to manage through the more usual and the tricky situations. With the ability to accept and embrace whatever emotional experiences may come, now it is critical that you know how to filter those experiences so the words and behaviors you express are of the highest vibration.

Emotional intelligence is a more recently coined term, but one could argue the concept has been in existence since the creation of mammals. Growing up, I like many others was measured by my book and intellectual intelligence. I was judged for emotional outbursts, but my intelligence was never measured by how well I understood and/or could manage my emotions. Nor did anyone teach me what "managing my emotions" was or how to do it.

It seems odd that with so much research completed on the brain that emotional intelligence wasn't a concept that was explored sooner. We know from research, that the rational and emotional part of the brain lie in the same place—the frontal lobe—and are at constant tug-a-war with one another. *"Neuroscientists are showing that the emotional and deliberative circuits in the brain are in constant interaction (some would say struggle), and the former, for better or for worse, often holds sway. What's more, with each new study it becomes clearer just how quickly, subtly, and powerfully our unconscious impulses work. Flash a picture of an angry or a happy face on a screen for a few hundredths of a second, and your amygdala instantly reacts—but you, your conscious self, have no idea what you saw."*

As if our impulses aren't challenging enough, we also now know that our brain develops over time. The part of the frontal lobe that processes emotions is more developed at an early age compared to the part of the frontal lobe that processes reason and logic. That may be the most fascinating part of research in this area—we are more emotionally than logically enabled out of the gate and yet we never learn that point, the importance of it, or how to harness its power.

In fact, we almost take the opposite approach. We spend years through schooling and jobs learning how to be more "logical", how to reason to make critical decisions. *"...for executives taught to methodically frame problems, consider alternatives, collect data, weigh the options, and then decide, cultivating emotional self-awareness may seem like a dispensable exercise—or at least not a critical tool in decision making."* We teach people that to be successful it is more important to think logically. We have created a paradigm that supports the belief that leaders developing emotional intelligence, or other "soft skills" may not only be useless but frankly speaking a waste of their time. Ouch.

When much of our life is experienced through interactions with other life - humans, animals, nature - how can we overlook the vitality of how emotions play a lead role in how we relate, connect, and influence? Arguably critical components of a great leader. But therein lies the problem. We drank the *Kool-Aid*. We have accepted leaders with little to no emotional intelligence for years and as a result we have more disingenuous executives and in some cases tyrants rather than true leaders running our companies.

An even heavier weight to carry, we have forced our employees to adapt to these leaders - accepting that we tolerate low Emotional IQ and even promote it. We have set the example that rising through the ranks has little to do with your emotional intelligence so why would anyone with ambition to become an executive invest the time in building their own Emotional IQ. I'll tell you why we should invest the time. For ourselves, it only enriches our lives. Knowledge is power and to be empowered to know you can understand and manage your emotions and emotional experience means you have more insight and influence into how to create your own happiness. In corporate America, without emotional intelligence and other soft skills, our world will continue to suffer. Simon Sinek calls them "human skills" instead of soft skills, and I whole-heartedly agree. We must be willing to admit just how important these human skills are that we learn such as emotional intelligence, compassion, human kindness, vulnerability, and humility.

Though some may have desires to run a company of robots, I am still of the mindset that robots will never replace humans entirely and if they do, we are truly doomed as a species. If you are like me and want to keep the dream alive that humans can still evolve in positive ways, let's talk about how to become more emotionally self-aware and increase your Emotional IQ.

WHAT ARE MY EMOTIONS AND WHERE DO THEY LIVE?

To tap into the power of your emotions you must first learn what they are and where they live in your body. You can easily start to do this through a visualization exercise.

Find a place to sit quietly and undistracted. Uncross your legs, put your feet on the ground and take some deep breaths. Now imagine an emotion or an experience that made you feel an emotion. I like to start with more charged emotions like anger. For me, if I visualize a time when I was angry and I really take myself back to that moment and feel into what it was like to be angry I start to notice my jaw clenching. Fists start to form, my whole body feels rigid, and I can feel the weight of my teeth biting my tongue, so I don't scream. For me, this anger almost feels like an explosive rage. I can feel and see a dark volcano with steamy hot lava ready to burst out and pour all over my surroundings.

Keep working with the exercise through various emotions, anger, love, sadness, joy, anxiety and so on. Take note of where you feel it in your body and write it down. What exactly do those parts of your body feel? If you could put an image or color to it, what would it look like? What color would it be? Do you smell, taste, or hear anything? Do you feel your body temperature changing? Are your palms sweating? Is your heart pounding? What is your natural reaction to this emotion? Do you want to express it? Hide from it? Shove it down? Resolve it?

Everything that comes to you write it down. The more you get to know your emotions - what they are, where they live and how they feel - the more you can start to manage them. If anger usually results in you snapping and you want to learn how to not snap, you must first learn how to recognize it when the emotion is coming on. If your body starts to clench and fists start to form, you know anger is coming and likely a snap. You can learn to intervene with your own emotional experience and temper your response. It is easier said than done and it takes practice. You will likely have some ungraceful responses as you are learning this new skill, but ultimately if you can become the master of your emotions, in most cases you will be able to control them.

An important distinction to understand is learning to manage your emotions doesn't mean that feeling them is wrong or you should negate them. In fact, it is quite the opposite. To manage our emotions, we not only need to understand and get to know them, but we also need to accept them. In some situations, we will have ample time to understand and accept our emotional experience whereas in other circumstances we may need to quickly manage them.

We can't help that we feel things - our emotions are a natural part of our makeup - but we can manage how we react to emotional triggers. The best trick I have learned for managing my emotional experiences in those quick scenarios is using my breath. Whether I am in a meeting and know someone isn't being truthful or am in a one on one with a leader who is berating me, taking a few deep breaths to help me accept the situation and my feelings about it for what it is while also calming my emotional experience helps ensure that my response is less emotionally "charged".

When you have the gift of time to process your emotions more thoroughly, there are other exercises you can use to help you understand and accept your emotional experience and manage how you respond. Below is a list of some of those practices:

- Take a walk; just moving from your current place to another spot will help if you don't have time for a walk
- Visualization and/or meditation
- Working out; whether lifting heavy weights or centering in yoga, physical exercise can be very powerful in processing emotions
- Go out into nature
- Try to gain perspective; think of something else that can help you put your current emotional experience into a greater context that might help you see a mole hill instead of a mountain
- Talk to a trusted friend/loved one
- Listen to music
- Journal

There are so many tools available to you, the key is acknowledging that taking the time whether a few seconds of deep breaths or an hour long walk, is worth the time and effort to help increase your emotional intelligence.

THE EMOTION THERMOMETER

One of my favorite tools to use as an everyday practice is what I call the "emotion thermometer" or taking your emotional temperature. I have a great passion for my *morning time.* I work east coast hours, so I am already up early, but I carve out the time for me to check in with myself. I pour my cup of coffee and sit down at my desk to take a few deep breaths, flip to my quote of the day, and open my work journal. I like journals that prompt certain questions to me - what are my three priorities for the day, what is the most important of all three, why is it important etc. But my favorite one is, "how am I feeling?"

Taking inventory of how we are feeling helps us determine how to best manage our day including our emotions. For instance, on days when I am feeling rested and energetic, I may take on some of my bigger tasks for the week and work a longer day. Inversely, if I am feeling exhausted or down, I take note of a few things. First, if I have the flexibility to move a few meetings or rearrange my schedule to take the more challenging meetings early on so I can have an easier afternoon I do so. If I don't have that luxury, which often happens, then I at least take note of how I am likely to respond to things when I am feeling more down and tired. I know I can be more snippy or not as focused so I can choose to place more attention in my meetings on taking some slow breaths and pay close attention to the words I speak so I can manage my emotional state in a more mature manner.

By checking your emotional temperature each day, you not only increase your Emotional IQ but being aware of and managing your emotions starts to become second nature and a part of how you live each day. At some point, much of your emotional awareness and response comes naturally and you won't have to think so much about it. That doesn't mean we don't still practice, because without practice we can lose those skills. If a daily inventory via a journal isn't your style you can add a reminder to your phone to ask you how you are feeling each day. You can also download apps like Calm that will prompt you with similar reminders and a chance to quickly type in a response or click on the words that resonate most with how you are feeling. Even just that quick check in will help you become more aware of your emotions.

PLAY IT ON REPEAT

Over time you will begin to recognize patterns and triggers. These are great indicators on your path to increasing emotional intelligence. One such trigger that may even be a universal one is when you are worked up and someone tells you to "calm down."

Pretty much everyone I know that hears that phrase when they are worked up gets triggered by it and the exact opposite effect takes place - we get more worked up and less calm. It is such a strange phenomenon but recognizing that it is triggering for you and likely for many others can help your emotional intelligence.

For yourself, knowing that the phrase might trigger you, you can prepare yourself or even recondition yourself to have a different response to that statement. If you want to recondition your response the next time, you're feeling worked up about something, you can do two things. First, you need a place, a sound, an object - something that does calm you that you can use to help recondition your response. Once you have identified what that is - playing a song/sound that calms you, lighting a candle, looking out the window at nature, call forward that statement in your mind. Say it over and over in your head or even out loud while also listening to your calming song/sound, or whatever you choose that calms you. Keep saying the statement in combination with experiencing your calming activity until you feel calm. Don't rush the process, it is critical that you continue with the exercise until your muscles relax, your breath slows, and you feel calm. No guarantees that you will feel completely calm the next time someone says it to you, but I would put money on you having a far less charged response.

For others, knowing someone's triggers gives you a gift. You have awareness of a vulnerable place for someone which means they trust you enough to let you see that part of them. If you truly desire to be an emotionally mature human, use this gift with great care and do your best to stay away from the triggers. If you see someone you care about, get triggered, you can also use it as an opportunity to hold space for and/or be a support system for them as they move through their emotional response to that trigger.

EMOTIONS IN THE WORKPLACE

In my experience, a typical display of emotions in the workplace often looks like this:

A meeting is taking place, two people emerge with opposing agendas, rather than seek to understand and find compromise or resolution they begin to use intimidation tactics to get under each other's skin, the antagonize one another back and forth like a ping pong match as the rest of the room sits patiently awaiting the temper tantrum display to end. Eventually one of them caves to the pressure of immature comments and snaps. They raise their voice and say something wildly unprofessional bringing the "fight" to a screeching halt as they realize it has gone too far and the discomfort of the audience to this display of emotional unintelligence is now unbearable. Someone finally chimes in, diffuses the argument, and moves the meeting forward or to an end. Everyone leaves the room feeling like there is a layer of gunk they are now carrying out with them into the rest of the workday. Most likely no one reports it or says anything to the two parties. Work and life move on, and people eventually forget it happened, until it happens again.

What is this kindergarten? When it comes to emotional intelligence, sadly, often it is kindergarten in the workplace. We haven't learned anything since we were 5 years old to help mature how we manage our emotions. As a result, we see grown adults still working out their childhood traumas, lack of emotional awareness, and power plays without any consideration to how it is impacting their own well-being and worse those who must endure it as a bystander. And yet again by tolerating the behavior we inadvertently accept it is a normal leadership behavior when in fact most of us would reasonably agree it is an unacceptable behavior. So why don't we correct it?

There are times where an executive may be in such a meeting and defuse the situation quickly. But what happens if the two most senior people in the room are the ones bantering? Most people don't feel comfortable intervening or feel they have the skills to help defuse the situation. I have seen this scenario play out time and time again. Earlier on in my career, I too was uncomfortable intervening. Now as an executive, I feel responsible for setting the tone and ensuring that people feel the workplace is a safe and mature place to converse. As a result, I have learned how to stay calm in those situations and use simple, non-emotional, unbiased responses to help call out the unacceptable behavior in a professional way while moving the meeting forward. An example of a statement I have used many times is, "This interaction is not serving the meeting and it seems you two have unresolved views that would better be managed offline. Let's move on." I wish I would have felt more empowered to intervene when I was younger. There is no reason for unprofessional banter in the workplace and we all should feel empowered to set the tone and lead by example.

Separately, I have often called the individuals who partake in situations like these and addressed it head on with them offline. I use it as a time to connect and build stronger trust with the person, not as a chance to make them feel bad about what they did. We all have bad moments and someone who is willing to call you out in a non-threatening manner while also holding space for you to choose to be different in the future is part of what makes emotional intelligence such an important skill. It is compassion, human kindness, and courage to stand up for what is best for the greater good.

If we took more care of our emotions - understanding them, thoughtfully expressing them, and holding space for others to do the same - our world and our companies would be a more enjoyable and safer place to be. Hopefully this chapter has given you some inspiration and tools to put practices in place that can support our continued journey to greater emotional intelligence.

7
FAILURE

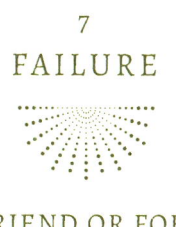

FRIEND OR FOE?

"The success of failure is to fail without feeling like a failure." —Sasha Stair

---

Have you ever noticed in the workplace that people are full of the "failure phrases" but never seem to want to talk about real failures? Executives will say, "We need to build a culture of failing fast," or "Fail forward," or my personal favorite, "Innovation requires us to be comfortable with failure and even promote it." But when push comes to shove, executives are terrified of failure. What if my scorecard turns red? What if my bonus is impacted? What if I get fired? If executives are so fearful of failure, how in the world are they ever going to inspire a culture of failing fast?

More so, what about the fact that we do fail in companies - every day. Are we really talking about those failures? Through agile methodology, there is a practice called a "retrospective" that allows you to go back and think about all the things that went well and didn't go so well for an initiative. Ultimately once all participants have expressed their views, you create an action plan on how to do better next time. This is most certainly a good start, but what about the bigger failures? What about the efforts that cost millions of dollars that end up being a throw away? What about startups or small organizations that go south? What about the CEO who can't get the company to evolve to its next phase of life? When was the last time you heard a story at work about those kinds of failures and what the leader truly learned because of failing and how they have changed their plans, behaviors, actions - if at all - post failure?

MY GREATEST FAILURE

I had the privilege of running a nonprofit years back. I had served as a volunteer and ultimately our fundraising chair on the Board when I was asked to take over as executive director. I was young, in my mid-twenties, and I had never run an organization before - well aside from the summer camp I ran out of my parents garage one year. I knew walking into the executive director role that there was a lot I didn't know. I had a Board stacked with great people. They were diverse in their backgrounds and all extremely talented, caring, and dedicated leaders both in their companies and on our Board. The Founder of the organization remained on the Board as well. I think that was mistake one for me, agreeing to allow the Founder to stay. As much as I adored, respected, and admired the Founder, I had heard and read about *Founders Syndrome* and how it can significantly impede an organization from moving on to its next phase.

One of the first decisions the Board made was to disband the half-marathon fundraiser we hosted twice a year. I advised greatly against this vote because the funds collected from these two events comprised 80% of our operating budget. I appreciated the confidence the Board had in my sales/fundraising background to help create and promote new programs that would provide new sources of income, but I was deeply concerned with us cutting our other program too soon. I had proposed that we continue with the marathon program until we had reached at least 50% replacement of those funds from new programs, then we could start to look at a plan to retire. But I didn't fight hard enough and because the Board trusted the Founder so keenly, the decision was made to stop hosting our marathon program.

Just like any leader in my situation, I got to work quickly on ideas for new programs that the Board could consider that would bring in quick but also sustainable funding. The ideas I presented were all accepted, and we moved forward with two main programs to start. We saw momentum very early on from both but a few months in I could see the writing on the wall. Even though these programs would work, we may not have enough runway to make up the funds fast enough.

I thought long and hard about what my next steps would be as ED. It seemed so doomsday and too soon to plan for the worst, but I felt some push inside of me to create such a plan. I created Plan A, B, and C. Plan A was to keep pushing the new programs and host a blowout end of the year event where we had the potential to raise our entire operating budget in one night. In our following Board meeting, I expressed that if we were going to pump the gas, we needed every Board member to dedicate time, resources and gather support for our end of year event. It was a big donor event at a private home, we had a live and silent auction, a celebrity host, students from our programs who came to share their stories of their traumas and how our programs changed their lives, in some cases even saved their lives. The event was amazing, but it didn't bring in enough revenue to hold us over.

On to plan B: stop paying myself as ED and save as much reserves as possible to help try to bridge the gap while also creating a *Season of Giving* video campaign. We brought in a professional videographer pro bono to film our story. Board members, students from our programs and volunteers all gave time to create this incredible video that brought tears to most anyone who watched. I also provided scripts for the Board members to create their own 30-60 videos to send to friends, colleagues, and family to support the cause during our *Season of Giving*. I was sure Plan B would be enough to pull us through to the new year and give us hope for either reconsidering bringing back the marathon runs or other programs that could also help with fundraising. Sadly, it wasn't enough, and we were at the point that I couldn't pay our Program Manager and as a result we couldn't keep the talent. My heart broke again as I watched one of the most talented and caring professionals walk away, knowing our programs would be at risk and at the same time felt Plan C coming to life.

Plan C which I had created as the final call was to step down as ED. Whether our failure as an organization was my fault entirely or partially, I hadn't done my job to its fullest. I was unable to reach our goals and pull us out of the hole we were in. I wrote arguably the most passionate letter of my life (which I still have) to the Board notifying them of my decision, explaining my rationale, and laying out where I felt I and we as an organization went wrong, what was left and options to move forward including an option to close the nonprofit if the Board felt they didn't want to choose the other options. In the end, the nonprofit stopped providing services and ultimately faded away.

Even sitting here now writing about this failure, tears well up. It was the hardest and most profound professional experience of my life. I learned so much about organizations, myself, working with others, how to truly manage a Board, and so much more. I hold myself accountable for the failure of that nonprofit l. I would have hated to fail with any organization, but this one was so close to home given my own traumas that attracted me to the organization for healing and ultimately led me on a journey of far more than just a safe place to heal. How could I have failed the one place that helped me heal so I could ultimately help others heal too? UGH. It kills me. Tears me apart inside into impossibly little pieces. And yet, it happened. It is a part of me and my journey as a leader and a human. We all have these stories. The experiences that didn't work out and broke your heart; professionally and personally.

Because I feel so compelled to talk about failure head on, I want to humbly share what I think I would have done differently if I could do it all over again. I want to preface with, it has been over 10 years since I was in that role and there is still so much, I don't know. So, who knows if my ideas would have even worked? But that important part of this exercise is to be open-minded, compassionate, and creative in thinking about what else I could have tried so I have those ideas in my back pocket for a rainy day. I also want to respect the leaders who were by my side at that time. I don't blame any of them and I trust we all did the best we could with what we had available to us back then.

USING SELF-REFLECTION TO LEARN FROM OUR FAILURES

So, lessons learned both in running the organization and the eventual demise of my leadership in the ED role. First, I had never led a Board before. I learned very quickly in my first meeting the importance of socializing concepts ahead of a meeting with the members. First, you don't want any surprises. If there are going to be conflicting views or someone who opposes your ideas, best to know up front so you can devise a strategy for how you will facilitate a respectful and inclusive dialogue to find a solution. Second, if possible, you want buy in. Walking into a Board meeting knowing that everyone is aligned on items that need to be voted on allows you to essentially have done your homework offline so you can focus the meeting on leveraging creative brains to solve other problems. In case you are wondering, I didn't do those things ahead of my first Board meeting and it was a cluster. I spent more time mediating, trying to divert people from rabbit holes, and determine if there would be any productivity at all. Part of me wondered if I would be better off calling it a day knowing it was a lost opportunity to get the Board members into a productive environment so we could leverage their skills, minds, and hearts.

Since that time, when I know I am going to present a new concept to a team or leader I socialize my materials ahead of time with peers and colleagues. I gather their feedback, make appropriate changes and then I begin to socialize in person with the team that reports into the leader I ultimately will present to. Why? Because whether they are in the room the day I present or not, their buy in will eventually either be required or only help the chances of my idea being successful. You want people on your side, and you also want people to tell you if your idea needs work. Without being able to remember, I would wager that all my greatest successes presenting to C-Suite executives have been because I included others in the process of both crafting and modifying my concept while also getting the hard questions ahead of time, so I knew how to answer them when the C-Suite member(s) asked.

Trusting myself which we discussed in the Self-Trust chapter is another impactful lesson. I knew in my heart that abandoning our main operating income source was a terrible idea. It seems obvious that it was a dangerous risk, but you would be surprised how easy it was for us to just let it go. The program was a lot of work, and it was challenging to manage our other programs when so much of our time was focused on the half-marathons. Still, like any other startup or small organization leader, you learn that even if you must work 100 hours each week you do whatever it takes to make sure the funding is there because without it you have nothing. Looking back, I wish I would have trusted my instincts and found a way to make it all happen –kept the half-marathon program and new programs to help augment our income.

Now, when I have self-doubt, I really take a closer look. When someone questions why I am doing something or disagrees immediately I think, my idea must be flawed. And maybe it is and that is okay. Or maybe it isn't, and the time is just not right. Or perhaps my framing of the message isn't quite right. Rather than just jumping ship, I take time to pause and reflect. Is there something I am missing that would help make this successful or do I still believe in it just the way it is, and I am going to continue to push forward? Regardless, I don't let one "no": stop me. Which after being in sales you'd wonder how I ever did back then, but hindsight is 20/20.

One last lesson for now, particularly for those who are in or will one day be in an executive director or CEO/president role. I allowed the Board to influence me more than I influenced them. I fully believe this was a mistake. I want to say that you almost have to be *bullish* in your approach. Not in how you communicate and influence but, in your heart, and with your plans. You can adjust if you feel along the way feedback is warranted but if you have been trusted by a Board to run an organization, then run it as you see fit. Relentlessly come back to your intuition and your higher knowing. Like we talked about, your inner voice knows how to guide you. You must only have the stillness to listen and the courage to follow its advice.

HOW TO FAIL WITHOUT FEELING LIKE YOU'RE A FAILURE

As an executive, the courage to listen to your inner voice and trust its advice is much more challenging. However, I still believe that as an executive you are brought to a role because you possess leadership, management, and other skills that the organization needs. Being anything less but true to yourself and the power of your abilities is shortchanging the company, your team(s), and yourself. That doesn't mean all tact and professionalism goes out the window. What it does mean is if you aren't prepared for heading into situations of conflict, differences in leadership style, and political agendas then you might want to look for a different job.

Being an executive is not easy, but it is a privilege to be in an executive leadership role. I could list a dozen attributes I believe we need in leaders to change culture and our world, but one stands out as a precursor to all the others. As Brené Brown says in many of her podcasts and writings, we need leaders who have the courage. If we truly want to change corporate for the better, the leaders who have the courage to be more open about our failures and not shy away from the details because they are "messy" are the ones who will open the gates. When I share with vulnerability about my failures, people gravitate closer. They feel a shared connection to their own stories, to your humanity, and the idea that just like you they too had failures. But those failures served as guides rather than dents along their journey to the top.

I also don't limit the interaction to sharing my own failure. One of my favorite practices as a leader to implement is the "how do we not do that again" talk. Once in a meeting on a tough project loaded with more political agendas than there are toppings for a baked potato, my team was getting berated and beaten up bad. I did what all leaders should do, took responsibility for the full actions of the team (which I knew included one of my team members lying to make the project look better off than it was), and held myself accountable for going back to work with the team on how to resolve the issues.

Offline, I took my manager and product owner into a private room. The look on their faces was of sheer terror. They knew I wasn't a "yeller", but I could tell they were feeling this might be the day Sasha explodes. We sat down and for both the purpose of letting the weight set in while also gathering my own emotions and logic I let us sit in silence for a few minutes. Then I said, "Well, that sucked. Let's talk about what went wrong and what we need to do to ensure that never happens ever again." They sighed and laughed with relief. Then we talked, drew on the white board, and connected as equals with shared responsibility on how we were going to make things better. I realized through that experience that people don't want to fail but they know they will. The key is when they do, they don't want to *feel* like a failure. That is such a poignant difference. It is ok to fail. But no one should ever feel like a failure as a person. It is a point I think we miss a lot in how we judge ourselves and how we lead and manage teams. Some leaders are just complete a**holes about failure, but others may not even think to call out just because we failed doesn't mean we are a failure.

People are complicated, but they are also so simple. They just want a safe space to grow, to fail, to succeed, to be who they are. We as leaders and managers can and must help them do these things by creating a safe container. A Harvard Business Review study revealed, sharing openly with teams has been proven to create more cohesive, high performing teams that are resilient in the face of challenges. What a gift we are given to have that power. We must take care of that power and our people. We must ensure that failure becomes a friend and not a foe and that takes more effort than just stating we need a culture of failing fast. It requires us to really talk about failure and our fears surrounding it - what is failure, what it's not, what it means to each person, and how we can befriend failure and our fears to help us on our respective and collective journeys.

8
RISE WITH INTEGRITY THROUGH THE REAL SHIT SHOW

"Integrity is choosing courage over comfort; choosing what is right over what is fun, fast or easy; and choosing to practice our values rather than simply professing them."—Anonymous

The "rise to the top" is not an easy one for most people. I have watched for years as many good people rose to the top on merit and then allowed fame and power to change them for the worse. I have also watched as people made poor decisions, stepped on others, sold their soul to the devil, and risked everything just to get ahead. It seems sad that it feels more rare than common to find the leaders who truly rose to the top with integrity. No shortcuts, no giving up their values, and most certainly not using others as a means to their own success. But they do exist and whether they are becoming the norm or still the minority, it is my mission to change that, and I hope you will join me.

Regardless of the environment, a beautiful and at times painful experience of rising with integrity is the change that occurs. Leading with integrity ultimately means you will have conflict with others that will not always end well. You will shed relationships along the way because as you stay on your path those around you who choose not to do the same will no longer fit. At times it can feel like a loss. A colleague or boss that was also a friend turns into someone you no longer speak to. Typically, those moments are hard. Sometimes they feel like a huge relief; a weight off your shoulders removed. But if you are anything like me, no matter how right the loss of the relationship, it never comes without grief and sadness.

At many companies, I have seen "integrity" used as a value you are measured against for your annual review. It always strikes me as a conundrum of how you rate someone on integrity when the scale is: does not meet expectations, meets expectations, or exceeds expectations. There has been much debate as to whether integrity can be measured in this manner or if it is something you either display or don't. Personally, I believe it is both. There are basic morals and ethics I feel are standard; being honest, not breaking laws, doing the right thing (especially when it is hard), etc. There are also other behaviors that I feel range from right to wrong with a gray area in the middle.

For instance, do you accept a meal as a business meeting and not pay for your food and drink? I know some leaders who have never accepted anything from a vendor to ensure there was never any question. It is a trait I admire but not one I have followed in my career. Then comes the gray area. Are you accepting the meal with the intent to play quid pro quo or are you able to maintain moral ground and accept the meal without any feeling of obligation to do business with the party based just on the meal, the baseball game tickets, or the sponsorship to a conference? There are many instances that we will face decisions in our career whether as simple as a meal with a vendor or more complex like an investigation into a colleague. The key is to understand beyond the shared standards of moral and ethics we have as a society, what are your personal values that you want to uphold as a leader and human?

I have definitely made some poor decisions and mistakes in my career. And, along the way I have built a set of values that I carry with me to remind me in hard situations not to let the scenario sway me in the wrong direction. It is in those circumstances that I believe our true integrity is brought into question. Our desires and our innate wanting for there to be a lack of conflict that places us in the "stuck beneath a rock and a hard place" can leave us in incredibly uncomfortable positions where we must look in the mirror and ask ourselves not what is best for our careers but what is right.

I recently have shifted my values from more basic language to fun, engaging mantras that help remind me in moments of challenge to live my values. Whether you end up taking some of these or creating your own, I highly recommend you know your own personal values. In fact, I borrowed one from the military.

1. Show your cards - when it comes to being part of a team, it is important for us to be transparent, vulnerable, and honest with ourselves as much as with our colleagues. Showing your cards means you don't play Poker and hold your hand, you lay down your cards, admit what you've got and what you don't and be willing to accept help or alternative options to do what is best for the team and company.

2. Even if it hurts me, if you need me, I am coming - this is the one I borrowed and I love it. Even if I may not benefit, or I may lose something, no matter what if my teammate needs me, I will put my own agenda aside and show up to help them because it's what's right for the greater good. It speaks to more than just being dependable or reliable, it means you are in the trenches with your people, your peers, your teams, your leaders.

3. Practice what you preach - if I am asking someone else to do it, I better be willing to do it too. It also speaks to following through, if you say you're going to do it, do it.

4. Lead by example - it is a tried-and-true mantra for a reason. People watch your moves, they look to you for guidance, to see how you will respond - especially when things get tough.

5. Everyone is a teacher and a student - In any given situation we can both teach and learn - if we keep that open mind, the world is our oyster.

6. Do what you know is right, especially when it's hard - ask yourself the question, can you lay your head down tonight to sleep? We know what is right by the law, company policies, societal social graces and we also know what is right by our book when faced with the more colorful scenarios. Have the courage to listen to what you know is right and act accordingly.

7. Spread light - through truth, compassion, inspiration, passion, joy, positivity, respect, love, human kindness - be, shine, and share the light with everyone and everything.

8. Own it - know yourself - your strengths, weaknesses, blind spots - and own it. Be real, be you, and own it. Be responsible for your actions and own them. Hold yourself accountable and own it. Admit to your mistakes and own it. Accept the choices you make, accept the life you create, accept all that is and will be, and own it.

DON'T COMPROMISE YOUR VALUES FOR SUCCESS

It is one thing to give examples of the types of values, ethics, and morals we should have in business and life, but the real lessons occur when the reality of those hard situations are brought to our front door. On more than one, heck more than a handful of occasions, I have been presented with scenarios that either offered me immediate success or the ability to not wrong a leader who had some level of power to potentially make my career better or worse.

I consider myself an ethical person, but some of these situations left me in uncomfortable and seemingly impossible positions. Regardless of what move I made; I knew there would be consequences. Whether I acted in favor of the person who was asking me to either be unethical or stand by and watch them be immoral, acted against them, or stayed quiet, they all came with a price.

In each situation, I would find myself in the "moral dilemma" of debating in my head the impact of each option. Sometimes it was clear, and I knew which option I needed to follow, but it didn't make it any easier. In other situations, I struggled with leaving the situation alone or acting. I'd like to share an example of each of those with you to dive into the details of the emotional and psychological battle we as leaders go through when presented with these circumstances. I have encountered these examples at more than one company and will keep details as high level as possible to not reveal anyone involved other than myself.

THE REAL SHIT SHOW 101

Many of you know what I am referring to when I say the "intimidating and coercive" leader. It is the person (or in my case people because there have been many) who use scare tactics and false promises to coerce you into either doing or hiding their dirty work. In one example, I was asked to delete and falsify records as a cover up of sorts. At first glance, this one seems simple. It is an illegal activity so clearly the answer is no. And I knew there was no way in hell I was going to delete/falsify records. But what would I do next?

For many people in their careers, their job isn't just something they do because they enjoy their work. It is a source of income, a means to support a family, bills, your life. In those moments when you know the right decision is not to do it, but you are left with other concerns - what about my job? Will I lose it? What about reporting this person to HR? I don't want to put this person at risk, but they have put me and the company at risk, so am I wrong if I don't report it? I sat in a room with many others that day and watched the expressions on everyone's faces; cowering into their corner, shocked and stunned, the blank face that says it all.

Whether good, bad, or indifferent I was and still am a fairly ballsy leader. Without even thinking about the spiral effect that would take place once I opened my mouth, I told the leader in front of the group, "You are asking us to perform an illegal activity and I won't do it." Let's call this leader Frank. Frank's response hit me like a freight train, "If you don't, you no longer have a job working for me." Ouch. Now I am really stuck in the mud. I left the conference room and went back to my office. I don't know who was more nervous, me or Frank. I know he was concerned I would report it. I was terrified of both reporting and not reporting the incident. I was also terrified of what would happen if I didn't report anything but also didn't change the records.

Up until this point, I had really admired Frank and enjoyed working for him. I wanted to be like Frank. I saw a pathway to being in his role one day and felt I had found my "home" and my "place." Part of me sat in my office thinking, "you jackass, why did you have to go and ruin everything?" The crazy part was, if we didn't change the records, I don't think anything terrible would have happened. There was nothing illegal going on to begin with. Frank had been asked to cease an activity by the Board and instead told us to continue. Chances are if Frank would have fessed up to not following the Board's direction, given the nature of the situation being fairly benign he may have got a slap on the hand, but I doubt he would have been fired for the mishap. It was a "not the end of the world" scenario the way I saw it. Frank saw things differently. Maybe he felt his job was being threatened or he was trying to save face, or both?

I loved that job and my office. I had one of those old-fashioned pictures on my wall that a teammate had printed out for me that said, "Don't be mad at me because I said out loud what you all were thinking." Oh, the irony of reading that sign as I sat in my office replaying my comment, Frank's response, the facial expressions of my colleagues and energy in the room over and over in my head. I'm pretty sure I even hit my head on my desk a few times, like clicking my heels three times and hoping the universe would take me anywhere but where I was sitting at that moment.

Just like many other scenarios we encounter in our career, this one had layers of complexity. The company we worked for had just survived an actual scandal of money laundering just a few years before this incident. A part of me knew the company wouldn't tolerate any small scent of misconduct. I knew if I reported anything, chances are Frank would be packing his office. Thinking about that scenario broke my heart. Frank had moved here for this job, he had a family, a life. I saw him as a mentor and someone I really enjoyed working for. What would become of Frank and his family's life if anything happened? What would happen to everyone else in the office? Would they be questioned? Could they lose their jobs? Would we get a new leader we hated? Head hits the table again and this time a sigh of frustration spews out. UGH. How could one stupid moment lead to all these emotional upheavals and all the "what if's" running through my pulsing veins?

Here is what I did and what I wish I would have done (and there are far more options than just these two that one could choose from). I went to HR and reported the incident. Frank went packing. What I wish I would have done was go into his office and give Frank a chance to change his mind. Explain to Frank the impossible position he put me and the others in and offer to sit down and think of a better way to handle the issue. If Frank would have still said no then I could have acted, but I never gave him a chance to admit he made a mistake, had a bad moment, and to take it back before it was too late.

See, we don't talk in business school about the reality of what you will experience when you go into Corporate. We teach ledgers, statistical anomalies, balancing the books, what colors make a customer want to buy, different types of operation strategies, and how to organize a function. We don't talk about the shit you are going to endure and how the heck you are going to navigate through. We also don't teach people to build trust with their teams in a way that I would have felt safe enough to walk into that leader's office and have the conversation that I now wish I would have had. Well, welcome to *The Real Shitshow 101,* a class I may someday teach in a lecture hall but for now these pages will have to do.

HARASSMENT AND WHY PEOPLE DON'T REPORT

I have many debates with my husband as to how pervasive sexual harassment really is in the workplace and how we solve for both the real occurrences as well as the people who feel it is acceptable to lie about such a terrible offense. As someone who has been sexually harassed and abused, it is insulting to those of us who have survived and often not reported the incidents, that anyone would ever use those circumstances as lies for their own benefit. I do not take those stories lightly and I also do not take the reality of how much harassment occurs every day in companies, sexual or otherwise.

Most of my career has been in more male-dominated settings. Whether the industry or the level I played at, I am often the only female in the organization or on the leadership team. I have regrettably tolerated harassment both sexual and not for years by colleagues, bosses, vendors, and clients. At times I felt comfortable enough to stand up for myself and at other times I have endured disgusting and vile acts and found a way to move on. I debated myself for years on why I never reported any of the acts; verbal sexual offensive comments, offers to buy more from me for sexual favors, berating me whether in an office or a meeting, including disparaging words in how they described me while yelling, physically making passes at me or while threatening me (subtle and violent), filming, and stalking me. They were all terrible examples of people who needed to just grow up and be a better human.

I did report two altercations in my career. One of physical and verbal assault and the other of sexual harassment. The first was so scary that I quit my job and took no shame in citing the incident as my main reason for leaving, particularly after they refused to address it with the leader even though I had multiple witnesses.

The second was tougher for me. It was an ongoing harassment with a colleague we will call Darren. It was starting to really bother me because beyond the harassment Darren was trying to play political games at work to damage me as well. I went to HR and had the "hypothetical" conversation. After describing the detail and length of time this had been going on, our HR professional was very concerned. Though it was still my choice, they adamantly recommended I report it. A couple of my colleagues knew it was going on and so I sat down with them privately to get their thoughts. I was really leaning toward letting it go and if it happened again in the moment head on just addressing it with Darren.

I hadn't done that yet because Darren was careful, whether he knew it or not. He had chosen situations where it would have been uncomfortable for me to speak up. At a happy hour with other colleagues or at a work event with a vendor. Many probably would have still spoken up or smacked the person but I felt frozen. Like how I felt when I was sexually abused earlier in my life. Unable to respond or act because I am literally having a silent panic attack inside my body and all those feelings of being touched in ways that you don't want come rushing through your veins like a paralytic medication.

As I was speaking to my trusted colleagues one of them said something that completely shifted my perspective, "what if he is doing this to someone else or many others?" I wish someone could have taken an X-Ray or MRI of my body at that moment because I am sure my heart fell out of my chest. Now I was thinking not of myself but worried sick that Darren was potentially hurting other people. There was and never came to be any evidence of that, but I couldn't live with the possibility. So, I reported the three incidents to our ethical hotline.

What came next was a complete and utter cluster that still leaves me disappointed with how some companies manage these situations. Darren admitted to some, but not all, of the incidents. He claimed he was drinking and didn't remember, but also stated he believed if I said it happened it did. I had witnesses that saw my facial expression of discomfort but didn't see Darren touch me. There were people looking out for Darren that said he was never anywhere near me at a 40-person event in a small bar area. Ultimately, the company decided Darren would need to take additional training but remained in his role as an executive and we were both put back into the workplace to figure out how to coexist on our own - no warning, no guidance, no support.

A few of our top executives sat down with me and said things that mortified me. "There are no witnesses that can corroborate your story, so we have no way of knowing you are telling the truth." How could they say this knowing Darren admitted to most of his actions? What felt worse was, even if the company chose not to act because they didn't have evidence, implying I am lying when Darren admitted to some of his actions baffled me and seemed cruel. The next one took the cake. "There are good people who make mistakes and bad people in the world who do bad things. I just think this is an instance of a good person making a mistake." And what about me who had to endure the harassment and now must go back to work with Darren every day in a small office where my job relies on me interacting with this person? What am I? Just a good person that got caught in a bad situation, oh well.

I went from feeling like I had done the right thing for not just myself but also others, to feeling like I had done something wrong. Worse, my boss had Darren's back, not mine. Claiming Darren had come crying to my boss about how bad he felt. For someone as manipulative as this guy, I am sure he brought the whole office stock of Kleenex with him.

I contacted two lawyers, both eager to take on my case. But again, here we are at *the Real Shitshow 101*. No one ever talks about the possibility of these terrible circumstances being pressed upon you. If I let one of the lawyers take the case, they both felt strongly I would win. But what does winning even look like? Clearly, I wouldn't be working there anymore. I now would have the reputation of being the girl who sues companies. And what would I get out of it? Some money that depending on the amount may have helped me float until I found another job or if I was lucky could have prevented me from working at all. But I didn't want money. And I really like what I do, and I like to work. So basically, I am sitting on a winning case in a lose–lose situation. I didn't file. And I stayed with the company continuing to work with Darren. To his credit, he never harassed me again. Whether for good reason or fear of losing his job I will never know but at least it stopped. There is some solace in that.

Looking back, I would still make the same decision. For a while I thought it would have been better to tell Darren to back off or I would report it. But in truth, leaders should know better. Most companies require annual training on harassment so there really is no excuse for the behavior regardless of the type of harassment. Many in my shoes would have left it alone or handled it on their own. In most cases they wouldn't report because the fear of going through what I experienced is too real. It is why so many people don't report harassment or abuse. Fear of being emotionally injured further, fear of nothing happening, fear of repercussions, and so many more. But if we don't speak up, we are accepting what we tolerate.

DON'T RUIN THE VIEW

I recall when the *me-too* movement began, I had such mixed emotions because though I believe in speaking up and creating a better world, it pains me that we need big stage campaigns to handle such a basic issue. We shouldn't need a "movement" to get people to listen and understand that we just need to do and be better. For me personally, campaigns like that draw too much noise and not enough change. And yet, I also understand that without them the injustices are often left in the shadows.

Regardless of our experiences and how we choose to handle them, the key for me in all of it is to act with integrity and live your values, whatever you decide and however you move forward. Beyond the harassment, intimidation, and coercion that I and many others have experienced there have also been other opportunities that may have advanced my career or made me more part of the "in crowd" but they all came with a price of giving up my integrity which is too high a price to pay. The shortcuts can seem so tempting at times, the desire to rise to the top so alluring. But one day you will be at the top and when you look back at your story, you are going to want to feel proud of each chapter. You will want to be the leader that made good decisions when times were tough, who put others before themself, and who chose to take the path less traveled. It may have been a longer, windier road but the view at the top is that much more beautiful and worth every struggle, set back, and hard decision.

Most of all, remember that no title, company, salary, or opportunity will define your worth. Only you get that power so don't allow the shiny objects to pull you off course and take away that power. When we move on from this world, no one is going to care if you made a ton of money or had the CEO title. People remember how they felt in your presence – how you impacted their lives. Be the kind of leader you have always wanted to work for and aspire to be. Be the leader who is known for doing the right thing rather than needing to be right. Be the leader who makes the tough calls with humility and grace. Be the empathetic leader who people remember for their heart, inspiring conversations, and care for their people's livelihood. Afterall, those qualities are what defines a great leader not their title or pay.

9
LEADING AN AUTHENTIC LIFE

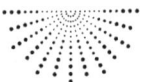

"Authenticity is the daily practice of letting go of who we think we're supposed to be and embracing who we are." —Brené Brown

I feel blessed to live and lead during a time where authenticity seems to be embraced rather than judged. I ache for those who have had to suffer in the dark, unable to be who they are for so long. I talk about moving from shadow to conscious leadership in, *Leading Through the Pandemic,* and I truly believe the pandemic gave us a gift. Working remotely and having to blend some level of your personal life into your work life has inevitably forced authenticity to the table. We no longer walk out the door and go to an office where we can put on a mask and be the "work version" of ourselves. Being at home makes it nearly impossible to be the same person you were in the office, and I for one think it is great.

Growing up in my career, I heard time and time again not to mix personal with professional. There are some instances where I do agree that certain things belong outside of work, but when it comes to who we are, our true personality, our authentic self – that is something that belongs everywhere, especially the workplace.

TRYING TO FIT IN

I worked through college, but my first "official" job out of college was medical device sales. I remember my first few years in the field having a level of young confidence that comes with being in your early twenties, combined with that feeling of "what the hell am I doing?" Like a child watching their parents to observe acceptable behavior, I watched my peers in the industry and started to work to mold myself to be more like them. The industry was very male dominated, so in many cases part of my molding was being more masculine, or so I thought. I had convinced myself what masculine was; abrasive, pushy, cut-throat, tough, strong voice, strong handshake, competitive, conniving, strategic, do anything to win, etc. I dressed in black and navy, mostly wore pant suits unless I was in scrubs. I wore heavier make up to seem older than I was and even at 5' 9", I stretched to stand taller in operating rooms.

As I close my eyes and bring back these memories, it almost plays out like a movie in my head. One that I laugh at, in the most loving way possible. I was so naive and so lost. But again, business school doesn't teach you how to "be" in the business world. You learn a few tricks on how to present and work with a client, but no one talks about what your identity and brand is and means. We don't teach people how to discover who your authentic self is and express it in a healthy way.

So, there I was, all of 22 years old trying to find my way in the world. Though I felt the need to mold myself to be more like my competitors, I also intuitively knew to be different. I was naturally more caring, emotionally mature, and hardworking. After a case in the operating room, if I saw trash on the ground, I would often pick it up on my way out and throw it away. People, including my bosses, would always ask me what I was doing. I was taught as a child to help, to pick up, to leave things better than you found them. I didn't even think about it, I just did it. The nurses and operating room staff noticed and appreciated it. What I didn't realize early on was nurses often make many of the purchase decisions in a hospital, so in helping them I ended up helping my success.

I also showed up early and stayed late. I took advantage of the opportunity to teach hospital staff continuing education for credits to increase my knowledge while also building stronger relationships with my customers. I was more patient and inquisitive than my competitors. I would ask questions to better understand why doctors made the decisions they did based on the nuances of each case. The more I gauged their thought process, the more I could engage in thoughtful dialogue that ultimately gained their trust and their business.

On one occasion, because I had shown up early and had built such trust, a well-known doctor at Georgetown University Medical Center helped me see just how different I was and how much it mattered. That day, the sales rep for my competitor that had 100% of Georgetown's business at the time was late to a case. He showed up that day in his normal entitled way, smiling as he walked past the nurses with that fake cartoon sparkle on his teeth that makes a ding noise as he winks. He strolled into the case as if his tardiness was of no concern and pushed me aside to get close to the surgeon. In medical device sales, you often walk a surgeon through the operation of a device. There are so many devices on the market, and they change often so it is impossible for doctors to know every in and out of each device. As sales reps we are trained to understand the engineering behind our devices and the anatomy associated to the need for our devices so we can best answer questions and be a trusted advisor to the doctor as they use the device on a patient. As this sales rep begins to walk over to the shelf to grab his device, the surgeon turns to me and says, "Do you have that stent with you so we can see what all the hype is you've been talking about?" I had been calling on the doctor for months now and he was known for being set in his ways – he rarely tried new devices. He did things a certain way, always had, same devices, same techniques and I was warned it may have been a lost cause for me to get him to try this stent. I was speechless and jumping up and down like a little kid inside as I calmly yet confidently replied, "Yes I do, would you like to give it a try today?"

The surgeon used my stent that day and saw the quality of life it would bring to his patients. So much so that he had the sales rep take back all those stents that were stocked on his shelves and restocked with my company's comparable, yet superior stent. The competitor sales rep stormed out of the operating room and as he walked down the hall, he punched a hole through the hospital wall. I kid you not. That day he was asked to leave the premises and the next time I saw a rep from that company it was someone else. The sparkling toothed sales representative had been banned from the hospital.

Once I came down off my natural high from the experience, I realized how significant being my authentic self was in that situation. I wasn't even trying to sell that day, not directly at least and yet through my natural instincts and behaviors, I increased our sales that day and for months to come by a credible amount while also knowing patients would likely be more comfortable and have less procedures. Georgetown was our top client in the territory and the stent was one of our most profitable devices. Sadly, that day wouldn't be enough for me to truly embrace all parts of myself, but it was the catalyst to start accepting myself more and the beginning of a beautiful journey to leading with authenticity.

BREAKING DOWN AND BREAKING THROUGH

I wish I could tell you whether for yourself or your children that there is a way to get through a corporate career without break down moments but like the rest of life, it just doesn't work that way. There is a sweetness that you can only taste if you have felt the bitter bite first. I recall an evening in my mid-twenties when I thought I had hit rock bottom. I did not turn to drugs or alcohol. I watched what alcohol did to my grandmother and father and refused to repeat their cycle. Though I wasn't diagnosed or being treated for it, I am sure I was depressed. I remember being in my apartment and looking in the mirror, hardly recognizing the face staring back at me. It was so distorted from all the layers and layers of illusions, stories, excuses, traumas, pain and suffering I had painted on like war paint.

Up until this point, I had shared very little with only a handful of people about my sexual abuse traumas. I hadn't talked to many people about anything really that was deep inside, not even myself. I titled this book *The Inside Job* because I believe whole-heartedly that the most important journey, we will take in our lifetime is the discovery and healing of self. Without it, we can't really evolve much. We repeat patterns and cycles, but we don't truly move forward. I believe everything starts and ends within us and everything we need is also within. So, if that is the case then the work we must do to heal ourselves so we can heal Corporate, and the world is in fact an inside job.

That night, I knew I didn't want to give up, but I also knew I couldn't keep living the life I was living. I laid in a shower drenched by more tears than tap water and I couldn't see a way out. It was the lowest low of my life and I almost took my own life. A friend showed up like a divine angel and stopped me. When I woke the next morning, I knew my life depended on me making significant changes. As I had cracked open my heart to allow the truth to pour out, I realized like any other human, I had two choices. I could bottle it all back up, pull myself together and move forward falsely believing I would never "break down" like that again or I could do what most people are too scared to do; face the pain and suffering head on. No running or hiding from it. Time to face the music and dance. Admit my role in everything; my choice of continuing the suffering when it wasn't required, my decisions to hurt others to protect myself, my irresponsible choices that unintentionally hurt others and myself, accepting and playing the role as victim. These were hard pills to swallow. Most people pack up and walk away from facing them because it feels awful. Sitting in and moving through our pain is terrible and it is also liberating. We must only have the courage to face ourselves in the mirror and see it all, accept it all without judgment and then choose what we want to do next.

For the following seven years or so after that night, I went into the depths of my soul searching for recovery, healing, and answers to who I really was underneath all those layers. I'm one of those "go big or go home" types, so I did it all. I was in therapy, I read every self and spiritual growth book I could find, hired a life coach, I went on self-development retreats, and I completed the Al-Anon program. I left corporate thinking that was the problem (it wasn't). Nevertheless, I found myself immersed in nonprofits volunteering my time to help others who were also suffering. I realized a year or so into this self-exploration that the answers and healing I was seeking was not going to be a "quick fix". I think many people want the quick fix. They start the journey and because you can't fully heal overnight, they eventually give up and go back to their comfort zone of pain because it is faster, easier, and more known. Looking back, I often wonder what kept me moving through the process rather than reverting backward. I believe there are a few things that were critical to my success and for any journey of self-healing.

My life coach was a critical pillar of strength for me. And I wouldn't say it was because she was a life coach, though that helped. It was more who she was as a person and our soul connection. Finding the right person who can help hold you accountable and remind you to trust the process and keep going is so vital. There will be more days than not that you will need to hear someone else say those words. I will forewarn you, the phrase "trust the process," will eventually make you want to throw something at a wall, but those words are truly so poignant and in time you will come to embrace them like a close friend.

I also was able to see early on how powerful perspective can be. You will have small wins or breakthroughs often. It is so important that you celebrate them, no matter how small, because that energy of seeing the small steps of change and honoring them will help keep you hungry for more. I noticed, the more I persevered the easier getting through hardships became. Circumstances that used to bother me elicited a less severe response and I was able to move past them much faster. I started to feel that liberation I referred to – the feeling that you are freer in your own life. We all have the tools available to free ourselves from our own chains, but we often don't talk about or teach people how to use the tools let alone that we even have that power.

What saddens me more is I feel we have built a world that thrives off this point. If we are scared, feel disempowered, and easily controlled then corporations, organizations, media, and administrations can take advantage and benefit while we ultimately lose. We have made certain things so easy – fast food, access to information, same day delivery, on demand everything – that it is even easier to avoid the hard stuff. But each of our lives depend on us saying yes to the inside job. Saying yes to have the courage to stand up to the status quo and both embody and inspire a different way – a better way. The world needs us to heal ourselves so we can spread that healing across so many parts of our humanity that continue to suffer. The future of our world and humanity is relying on us to remember that it only takes one person. One ripple in the water to expand out and change the world. It isn't easy, and it isn't a quick fix, but it is how we will shape the future. We must choose to do the work.

WELCOME BACK, YOU

If you are brave enough to say yes to the Inside Job and the journey of self-healing to live and lead more consciously, eventually you will start to recognize yourself more. Your true self is in there, you just need to dust things off so you can be fully seen. Even now, 13 years after I feel I really started my own journey, I am discovering new things about who I really am every day. If you are someone who feels like it's too late, here is what I will say to that feeling: with age comes some natural wisdom, so starting older does have some advantages. We all grow and evolve whether we want to, are trying to or not. Also, a little secret...we are all already on this journey. The question is are you willing to pay attention and lean into it more? One of the most challenging parts is the journey is never done. We will be on this road for the long-haul, but it is the road that keeps on giving and it has so much to offer if you are open to receiving.

About two years ago, I started writing a memo to my team every Monday. I shared an inspirational quote and a relative story with the intent of inspiring thought and self-reflection. I shared upcoming events and key information from our company and had a call out section to acknowledge my team members for their work. Over time, the memo evolved into a larger distribution list as people caught wind of the quote and story each week. I eventually repurposed the quote and story part into what I named "Monday Magic" and began sharing it more broadly. Each Monday, I take time in the morning to pick a quote that feels right and like a morning ritual, I sip my coffee and get to writing. The Magic gets shared internally on our intranet site and I also share it on LinkedIn and other social media outlets. My job has absolutely nothing to do with these magical notes and yet based on the responses I get from people; I would argue it is the most important thing I do. It never ceases to amaze me the replies I get back each week. It changes, always someone new, something that hits home with them and makes them stop and think or have a breakthrough. Each email I get back brings tears to my eyes because I feel like I am the luckiest person on the planet. Why? Because I am just being me. 100% authentically Sasha Stair and I get to live my purpose without even trying much. When I sit down to write, the words just pour out of me like they have been in an overstuffed drawer aching to burst out for years. I get to live my purpose in what feels like such a simple way with impacts that are profound beyond my imagination.

I recently received one such note after being out for three weeks recovering from surgery. I debated keeping up with the Monday Magic each week during that time but the first week I was barely conscious and the second and third week I was still so tired and felt like my body, mind and spirit really needed 100% of me focused on recovery. So, I took a break. When I wrote my first Monday Magic back from being off work, I received a note from a colleague:

"I did not know that you had surgery, but I figured that something isn't right as we haven't gotten the Monday magic for almost 1 month now...I personally enjoy reading your Monday Magics and it gives me an instant stress off from Monday madness. In the last hour, I have had to scourge through 100+ emails and already got tired from reading, responding, approving things, etc. And then your email popped up and it took me to think about other things I am grateful for, and how we take things for granted. Anyhow, I will start my first thing I am grateful for, and that is having someone in your professional life that reminds you of living life and why other things are important, not just work. So, I am grateful for you and for having you in our life and at our company. Thanks for sharing your thoughtful insights with all of us."

Tears...overwhelming feeling of butterflies inside consuming you up with light, purpose, and love. How can I ask for anything else when this may be the most meaningful thing I ever do? I feel blessed and it is all because I was brave enough to begin and continue the journey of leading an authentic life. Here I was for years trying to be someone else, or a different version of myself only to receive back negative energy; hardships, frustration, feeling isolated and unaccepted. Then one day, I flipped the switch and said, "screw it, I am just going to be me," and just like that *bazinga!* I get to be me, and the world loves me. It's really that simple? Yes, yes, it is. Don't let the hard stuff scare you, I beg of you to be brave with me. The gifts that you will receive on the other side are worth every ounce of growth pain – greater connection, a deeper sense of peace, liberation, more space for whatever you want to fill it with, adventure, co-creation, love, the list goes on and on. The world so desperately needs more authentic leaders, and I can't do this alone, so won't you please join me?

10
LEADING YOURSELF FIRST

"Everyone thinks of changing the world, but no one thinks of changing himself."—Leo Tolstoy

Hopefully by now, you can see the calling for focusing on your own healing and growth as a leader first. The reality is, most of us won't be able to just work on ourselves without also having to lead a team or organization, raise a family, and manage other responsibilities in life. But without commitment to ourselves at this deep and meaningful level, we are inhibiting our ability to live our best life and be a better leader. We can often feel selfish for prioritizing ourselves first, but the truth is this type of self-care is one that everyone benefits from and needs.

MAKE IT WORK FOR YOU

There is no recipe to follow for a self-discovery and healing journey. Though this book offers practical examples for how you can take on different phases, you will ultimately need to feel into what makes sense for you. Many of the books, teachers, retreats, and other resources out there on this topic are there to guide you. Only you can decide which guides and tools you want to bring with you, and which may not be your cup of tea.

You also don't want to boil the ocean, tempting as it may be. This is not a step by step, sequential, logical process. It is and will be messy, curvy, and feel like you are going backward or upside down in a blender at times. As I mentioned, this is arguably the most important journey you will take and so it should come as no surprise that it will have its challenges and take effort. Which is why it is so important that you make it work for you. Staying committed to the journey will take conscious energy so you will want to create conducive environments, choose compassionate companions, and reward yourself in little or big ways along the path.

For me, having daily practice is key to help me ground. I have my journal that I mentioned before, where I write down what I am grateful for and check in on my emotional and physical well-being before I start prioritizing my day. I personally like doing this with a cup of coffee and some music on. If the weather permits, the window is open and usually my

Maine Coon cat, Little Man, is trotting across my computer and desk as I take pen to paper. I work east coast hours and we have a huddle each morning (5:15AM my time) so I usually block 15-30 minutes right after that huddle for this practice. I am no longer in therapy, but I do still go on self-development retreats and read tons of books on growth, leadership, self, and spirituality.

Regardless of what practices and methods you choose, make sure that when you do them you overall feel good. You may have days where you just don't want to do them, or days where it is uncomfortable but that should be the rarity not the norm. If you hate doing something, forcing yourself to do it not only won't last but it won't provide the results you are looking for either. Just like anything else in life, figuring out your rhythms and cycles helps you determine what works for you and helps you stay committed.

BE PATIENT, OPEN, AND COMPASSIONATE

This is not like getting a degree. You won't get a piece of paper acknowledging your hard work four years later. This is a lifetime commitment. It also isn't really a "dip your toe in" kind of journey, at least not if you want to see the power of transformation. The journey will require you to be all in. Because of this, you will want to be patient with yourself and others.

One thing no one told me for a while which was hard to understand at first is, as you change everything around you will also change. This means that your life may start to look and feel different. Friends and colleagues, you once spent time with may not be the same people you surround yourself with as your true self comes forward. You may start to like different hobbies, dress differently, you may even start to like things you never thought you would. Try not to freak out, just embrace the change and wait for it...trust the process. You are on a train ride now. You are headed to the most beautiful and magical destination and some people are going there too, others may get off the train before you, after you, or even get on and off the train at different times. Your job is to focus on you and trust that things are happening for a reason.

I personally am very open with my stories. That isn't for everyone and that is totally okay. If you are like me, you may want to share your story more openly. Whether through intimate conversations with friends and family, on social media, or even through a book. Regardless of how you share, I do recommend you share. Even if it is in a journal only for your eyes to ever see. Being able to go back and reflect on your transformation is an awe-inspiring experience. Even better, if you feel you can, hearing other people connect to your journey, your pain, your joy, your discoveries are a beautiful experience. Often through my sharing, I have inspired others to take a leap, transform their own life, or just made their day better. No impact is too small.

When I volunteered and worked at Jeans4Justice, we used the ripple analogy frequently. Like a finger touching the water making one movement, it ultimately ripples out to create many movements and expands to reach more ground. Having a positive impact on just one person even just once would be worth the journey but the truth is, if you really commit to this path, you will impact so many more lives than you could ever imagine.

Being compassionate with yourself needs to just become a habit. We are way too hard on ourselves and usually for the wrong reasons. Being humble, self-reflective, taking responsibility for your actions, and holding yourself accountable are mature traits. Beating yourself up for not being good enough, rolling around in your own shit, and belaboring on how you could have handled a situation differently for months on end are unhealthy behaviors. We are human. We will make mistakes and we won't like every move we make. It is important that we reflect on these experiences for learning rather than punishment. We also need to cut ourselves some slack at times. We are allowed bad days and bad moments. It is in how you respond to and move forward from those moments that truly define you.

I have been going through the in vitro fertilization process this past year and the entire process is overwhelming and exhausting. Beyond the emotional, mental, and spiritual stress you endure, your body goes through absolute turmoil and hell. The hormone treatments are just delightful, and all the poking, prodding and procedures are enough to make you never want to see a medical office ever again. Like forever ever. My husband claims I have been fairly easy through the process and nowhere near the monster stories he heard from others. I think he is just being a good husband telling me what I want to hear. I have tried desperately to hold my tongue, take deep breaths, and manage this all as gracefully as I possibly can but in truth this process is anything but graceful. The level of expectation I have put on myself to uphold what I preach has been unattainable and at times I have had to remind myself to hold more self-compassion. Told you, lifelong journey.

THE INSIDE JOB PAYS WELL

Each experience we encounter will test what we have learned and push us to learn more if we are ready. Just think of it like Mr. Toad's Wild Ride at Disney. Some moments you are laughing and giggling having the time of your life and at other moments you want off the ride. "Sir, can you please stop the ride and let me off now. No seriously, right now. I don't care that we are in the middle of the willows, let me out now." Just remember, the inside job pays in priceless currencies of peace, freedom, purpose, and love, so stay on the ride.

In the past, a bad moment could take me down for a day, month or even a year, but now a bad moment is fleeting. I can see it, accept it, and move past it in seconds if I choose. It doesn't mean we don't process things that need time and space to work themselves out, it just means we can breathe life into the truth of the quote, "pain is inevitable, suffering is optional." We can choose to do the work so that we may be free to live a life with less suffering and more joy. When you reach the place where this is the norm rather than the exception, you don't even have to stop to smell the roses. The roses come to you. Doors open, things flow effortlessly, and the more you surrender the more shows up to support the life you most desire. It sounds ethereal and it is. I can't fully explain to you the magic behind why it all happens, all I can tell you is I've walked the road both with and without shoes on. I licked my wounds then ripped them open again. I've looked in the mirror and hated myself and kept looking until I could love and accept myself. I have been living the inside job for years and I am at a point where the inside job now works for me. I still have work to do, and I will stay the path, but if you are willing to dive in you will ultimately find that tipping point where it's no longer so hard and the benefits outweigh the effort. It is worth it, and I haven't met a person yet who regretted staying committed to that journey.

Even more beautiful, as we become closer to our true selves, so do others. That is leadership. Not giving up, following your intuition, and finding a way is leadership. Being vulnerable, authentic, and transparent is leadership. Allowing your true self to shine light on the world is leadership. The only way to that place is through. You can't go around, you can jump over, or limbo under. You must go through the dark to find the light. The good news is you are not alone. We are all in this together and if we remember that as we embark on our own journeys, we will begin to recognize others on their journeys. And in those unexpected moments when we notice another like ourselves, as if we are a character in a movie from across the room, we will bow our heads in recognition and honor of someone else who was as brave as us to accept the invitation to heal from the inside out.

ALOHA AND MAHALO

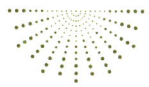

"Commit to the inner work and free yourself by finding yourself." —Michael Singer, The Untethered Soul

---

My wish for you is there are many things you can take with you on your journey from this book. And if for some reason it is only one thing that you take away, then let it be an aloha and mahalo from me. Love, that I openly share with you as an equal brave soul. I bow my head in gratitude for you as you continue your own unique journey. Know that you are seen, you are heard, and your life matters. Thank you for letting me share with you and for being my teacher and student. Writing this book has taught me so much more than I expected, about myself, life, and what's ahead.

Growing up, though I had stepbrothers they didn't live with us full time so mostly I was an only child. I remember having friends and interactions with family, but I also recall spending much of my time alone or with my cat, Oliver. Bless that poor cat for all he endured – me dressing him up, taking him for stroller rides, and sobbing all over him when I was sad. But I recall feeling like there was so much inside of me that needed to be shared but couldn't. Was there anyone there that would really listen or care? What would I share? So much of it seemed so dark and sad. What if people didn't like what I shared or even shrugged it off as rudimentary, inconsequential, or worthless. Feeling worthy was such a deep seeded trauma and trigger for me for so long. It took years for me to feel brave enough to really share. Which seems so odd looking back given I was in showstoppers, theater, musicals, sang with choirs and pep bands, played instruments – I was constantly on stage, front and center, and in the light. What I never realized was if someone would have shut off that spotlight, all that would have been left was darkness.

I had shoved my light so far down into the cave of my being, I never believed it would come out again. Not really. I could fake the light and be engaging and charming, just like my father was. But also, just like him, it would be an illusion. A mask to cover up all the things I didn't want anyone to know about or see in me, because what if they rejected my true self?

But the day came that holding in the darkness was too painful for me. Whether we want to believe it or not, the light will find a way to shine through. "We've all got both light and dark inside us. What matters is the part we choose to act on...that's who we really are." – Sirius Black — J.K. Rowling. One of my all-time favorite authors, J.K. proved that we can find light in the darkest of places. Little by little, as I opened myself up doing the work and sharing both my dark and my light, the universe showed up for me. The more I share over time, the more I receive back the most honoring, humbling, and heart touching sentiments from others. The world needs to hear our stories. Without stories our world is one-dimensional and without color. It is when we share our stories that the painting takes on life in color and dimension and if we look closely, we can see it moving.

When I worked with Jeans4Justice we had a catchphrase that I have carried with me and will always hold close, "We all have a story, the difference is how you live it." So how will you live your story? In the shadows, alone and hiding from your light? Or will you join me and start to color in the beautiful masterpiece that is your life with stories, healing, connection, and your true self shining brightly? The choice is yours and regardless of what you believe, I think we can all agree that life is too short to live in the shadows and not truly be living in our truth. Live your best life. Go all Oprah with me. I double dog dare you.

With all the magic, love, and light this universe has to offer,

Sasha

ABOUT THE AUTHOR

SASHA STAIR

Sasha Stair, known as the *spiritual warrior leader*, has a passion for helping people and companies grow through conscious and transformational leadership. With significant experience facilitating business transformation—from conception to execution—she brings emotionally intelligent leadership across people, processes, and technology to deliver results and drive innovation.

Known as a risk taker, Sasha has often chosen roles in her career that require self-transformation and reinvention. Consequently, she offers a unique skill set, spanning relationship cultivation and management, service delivery, strategy, sales, business growth, marketing, consulting, IT, and business operations with experience across multiple industries.

As an emotionally intelligent leader, her transparent and open communication style has provided a critical framework for cultivating trust, teamwork, and collaboration and has been an essential component of company performance.

Sasha is an engaging public speaker on topics ranging from conscious leadership to women's issues. Her unwavering commitment to fostering healthy relationships, both in the home and in the workplace, has drawn her to a number of volunteer roles, including with her alma mater San Diego State University's *FratMANners* and *SISSTER* programs and as an advisory board member for UC Irvine's Customer Experience.

Sasha considers herself a storyteller and has shared divine wisdom in two best-selling co-authored books, *Leading Through the Pandemic* and *Significant Women: Leaders Reveal What Matters most*. *The Inside Job* is her debut solo authored book and has already received incredible praise, including this jaw-dropping testimonial from an industry giant: **"A clear and witty guide for corporate leaders who are ready to reimagine the new wave of conscious leadership."** —*Keith Ferrazzi, NY Times #1 Best-Selling Author & Founder/Chairman of Ferrazzi Greenlight & Go Forward to Work.*

In 2012, AOL Patch and the California State Senate recognized Sasha as one of San Diego's Top 30 under

30 Leaders for her commitment to creating a positive impact in San Diego via her support of local initiatives for underserved women and girls.

Sasha is currently an executive in the financial services industry. She resides in Scottsdale, Arizona, with her husband, Matt, and their daughter Taylor.

LinkedIn: Sasha (Clines) Stair | LinkedIn

Made in the USA
Middletown, DE
03 May 2022

65132868R00086